MASTER THE™ DSST®

Principles of Finance Exam

About Peterson's

Peterson's® has been your trusted educational publisher for more than 50 years. It's a milestone we're quite proud of, as we continue to offer the most accurate, dependable, high-quality educational content in the field, providing you with everything you need to succeed. No matter where you are on your academic or professional path, you can rely on Peterson's for our books, online information, expert test-prep tools, the most up-to-date education exploration data, and the highest quality career success resources—everything you need to achieve your education goals. For our complete line of products, visit **www.petersons.com.**

For more information, contact Peterson's, 4380 S. Syracuse Street, Suite 200, Denver CO 80237; 800-338-3282 Ext. 54229; or visit us online at **www.petersons.com**.

ISBN-13: 978-0-7689-4469-3

Printed in the United States of America

10 9 8 7 6 5 4 3 2 1   23   22   21

Contents

Before You Begin.. **v**

How This Book Is Organized..v

Other DSST® Products by Peterson's.. vi

1   All About the DSST® Exam... **1**

What is DSST®? 1

Why Take a DSST® Exam? 1

DSST® Test Centers 4

How to Register for a DSST® Exam 4

Preparing for a DSST® Exam..4

Test Day 6

Principles of Finance Exam Facts..6

2   Principles of Finance Diagnostic Test.. **9**

Diagnostic Test Answer Sheet..9

Principles of Finance Diagnostic Test...10

Answer Key and Explanations..15

Diagnostic Test Assessment Grid 19

3   Principles of Finance Subject Review.. **21**

Overview 21

Financial Statements and Planning..21

Time Value of Money 31

Working Capital Management... 40

Valuation and Characteristics of Stocks and Bonds......................... 43

Capital Budgeting 54

Cost of Capital.. 58

Risk and Return 61

International Financial Management 64

Summing It Up 66

4   Principles of Finance Post-Test... **67**

Post-Test Answer Sheet... 67

Principles of Finance Post-Test 69

Answer Key and Explanations.. 89

Contents

Before You Begin

HOW THIS BOOK IS ORGANIZED

Peterson's *Master the*™ *DSST® Principles of Finance Exam* provides a diagnostic test, subject-matter review, and a post-test.

- **Diagnostic Test**—Twenty multiple-choice questions, followed by an answer key with detailed answer explanations
- **Assessment Grid**—A chart designed to help you identify areas that you need to focus on based on your test results
- **Subject-Matter Review**—General overview of the exam subject, followed by a review of the relevant topics and terminology covered on the exam
- **Post-test**—Sixty multiple-choice questions, followed by an answer key and detailed answer explanations

The purpose of the diagnostic test is to help you figure out what you know—or don't know. The twenty multiple-choice questions are similar to the ones found on the DSST exam, and they should provide you with a good idea of what to expect. Once you take the diagnostic test, check your answers to see how you did. Included with each correct answer is a brief explanation regarding why a specific answer is correct, and in many cases, why other options are incorrect. Use the assessment grid to identify the questions you miss so that you can spend more time reviewing that information later. As with any exam, knowing your weak spots greatly improves your chances of success.

Following the diagnostic test is a subject-matter review. The review summarizes the various topics covered on the DSST exam. Key terms are defined; important concepts are explained; and when appropriate, examples are provided. As you read the review, some of the information may seem familiar while other information may seem foreign. Again, take note of the unfamiliar because that will most likely cause you problems on the actual exam.

After studying the subject-matter review, you should be ready for the post-test. The post-test contains sixty multiple-choice items, and it will serve as a dry run for the real DSST exam. There are complete answer explanations at the end of the test.

OTHER DSST® PRODUCTS BY PETERSON'S

Books, flashcards, practice tests, and videos available online at **www.petersons.com/testprep/dsst**

- A History of the Vietnam War
- Art of the Western World
- Astronomy
- Business Mathematics
- Business Ethics and Society
- Civil War and Reconstruction
- Computing and Information Technology
- Criminal Justice
- Environmental Science
- Ethics in America
- Ethics in Technology
- Foundations of Education
- Fundamentals of College Algebra
- Fundamentals of Counseling
- Fundamentals of Cybersecurity
- General Anthropology
- Health and Human Development
- History of the Soviet Union
- Human Resource Management

- Introduction to Business
- Introduction to Geography
- Introduction to Geology
- Introduction to Law Enforcement
- Introduction to World Religions
- Lifespan Developmental Psychology
- Math for Liberal Arts
- Management Information Systems
- Money and Banking
- Organizational Behavior
- Personal Finance
- Principles of Advanced English Composition
- Principles of Finance
- Principles of Public Speaking
- Principles of Statistics
- Principles of Supervision
- Substance Abuse
- Technical Writing

Like what you see? Get unlimited access to Peterson's full catalog of DSST practice tests, instructional videos, flashcards, and more for **75% off the first month!** Go to **www.petersons.com/testprep/dsst** and use coupon code **DSST2020** at checkout. Offer expires July 1, 2021.

Chapter 1

All About the DSST® Exam

WHAT IS DSST®?

Previously known as the DANTES Subject Standardized Tests, the DSST program provides the opportunity for individuals to earn college credit for what they have learned outside of the traditional classroom. Accepted or administered at more than 1,900 colleges and universities nationwide and approved by the American Council on Education (ACE), the DSST program enables individuals to use the knowledge they have acquired outside the classroom to accomplish their educational and professional goals.

WHY TAKE A DSST® EXAM?

DSST exams offer a way for you to save both time and money in your quest for a college education. Why enroll in a college course in a subject you already understand? For more than 30 years, the DSST program has offered the perfect solution for individuals who are knowledgeable in a specific subject and want to save both time and money. A passing score on a DSST exam provides physical evidence to universities of proficiency in a specific subject. More than 1,900 accredited and respected colleges and universities across the nation award undergraduate credit for passing scores on DSST exams. With the DSST program, individuals can shave months off the time it takes to earn a degree.

The DSST program offers numerous advantages for individuals in all stages of their educational development:

- Adult learners
- College students
- Military personnel

1

Adult learners desiring college degrees face unique circumstances—demanding work schedules, family responsibilities, and tight budgets. Yet adult learners also have years of valuable work experience that can frequently be applied toward a degree through the DSST program. For example, adult learners with on-the-job experience in business and management might be able to skip the Business 101 courses if they earn passing marks on DSST exams such as Introduction to Business and Principles of Supervision.

Adult learners can put their prior learning into action and move forward with more advanced course work. Adults who have never enrolled in a college course may feel a little uncertain about their abilities. If this describes your situation, then sign up for a DSST exam and see how you do. A passing score may be the boost you need to realize your dream of earning a degree. With family and work commitments, adult learners often feel they lack the time to attend college. The DSST program provides adult learners with the unique opportunity to work toward college degrees without the time constraints of semester-long course work. DSST exams take two hours or less to complete. In one weekend, you could earn credit for multiple college courses.

The DSST exams also benefit students who are already enrolled in a college or university. With college tuition costs on the rise, most students face financial challenges. The fee for each DSST exam starts at $85 (plus administration fees charged by some testing facilities)—significantly less than the $750 average cost of a 3-hour college class. Maximize tuition assistance by taking DSST exams for introductory or mandatory course work. Once you earn a passing score on a DSST exam, you are free to move on to higher-level course work in that subject matter, take desired electives, or focus on courses in a chosen major.

Not only do college students and adult learners profit from DSST exams, but military personnel reap the benefits as well. If you are a member of the armed services at home or abroad, you can initiate your post-military career by taking DSST exams in areas with which you have experience. Military personnel can gain credit anywhere in the world, thanks to the fact that almost all of the tests are available through the internet at designated testing locations. DSST testing facilities are located at more than 500 military installations, so service members on active duty can get a jump-start on a post-military career with the DSST program. As an additional incentive, DANTES (Defense Activity for Non-Traditional Education Support) provides funding for DSST test fees for eligible members of the military.

More than 30 subject-matter tests are available in the fields of Business, Humanities, Math, Physical Science, Social Sciences, and Technology.

Available DSST® Exams

Business	Social Sciences
Business Ethics and Society	A History of the Vietnam War
Business Mathematics	Art of the Western World
Computing and Information Technology	Criminal Justice
Human Resource Management	Foundations of Education
Introduction to Business	Fundamentals of Counseling
Management Information Systems	General Anthropology
Money and Banking	History of the Soviet Union
Organizational Behavior	Introduction to Geography
Personal Finance	Introduction to Law Enforcement
Principles of Finance	Lifespan Developmental Psychology
Principles of Supervision	Substance Abuse
	The Civil War and Reconstruction
Humanities	**Physical Sciences**
Ethics in America	Astronomy
Introduction to World Religions	Environmental Science
Principles of Advanced English Composition	Health and Human Development
Principles of Public Speaking	Introduction to Geology
Math	**Technology**
Fundamentals of College Algebra	Ethics in Technology
Math for Liberal Arts	Fundamentals of Cybersecurity
Principles of Statistics	Technical Writing

As you can see from the table, the DSST program covers a wide variety of subjects. However, it is important to ask two questions before registering for a DSST exam.

1. Which universities or colleges award credit for passing DSST exams?
2. Which DSST exams are the most relevant to my desired degree and my experience?

Knowing which universities offer DSST credit is important. In all likelihood, a college in your area awards credit for DSST exams, but find out before taking an exam by contacting the university directly. Then review the list of DSST exams to determine which ones are most relevant to the degree you are seeking and to your base of knowledge. Schedule an appointment with your college adviser to determine which exams best fit your degree program and which college courses the DSST exams can replace. Advisers should also be able to tell you the minimum score required on the DSST exam to receive university credit.

DSST® TEST CENTERS

You can find DSST testing locations in community colleges and universities across the country. Check the DSST website (**www.getcollegecredit. com**) for a location near you or contact your local college or university to find out if the school administers DSST exams. Keep in mind that some universities and colleges administer DSST exams only to enrolled students. DSST testing is available to men and women in the armed services at more than 500 military installations around the world.

HOW TO REGISTER FOR A DSST® EXAM

Once you have located a nearby DSST testing facility, you need to contact the testing center to find out the exam administration schedule. Many centers are set up to administer tests via the internet, while others use printed materials. Almost all DSST exams are available as online tests, but the method used depends on the testing center. The cost for each DSST exam starts at $85, and many testing locations charge a fee to cover their costs for administering the tests. Credit cards are the only accepted payment method for taking online DSST exams. Credit card, certified check, and money order are acceptable payment methods for paper-and-pencil tests.

Test takers are allotted two score reports—one mailed to them and another mailed to a designated college or university, if requested. Online tests generate unofficial scores at the end of the test session, while individuals taking paper tests must wait four to six weeks for score reports.

PREPARING FOR A DSST® EXAM

Even though you are knowledgeable in a certain subject matter, you should still prepare for the test to ensure you achieve the highest score possible. The first step in studying for a DSST exam is to find out what will be on the specific test you have chosen. Information regarding test content is located on the DSST fact sheets, which can be downloaded at no cost from **www.getcollegecredit.com**. Each fact sheet outlines the topics covered on a subject-matter test, as well as the approximate percentage assigned to each topic. For example, questions on the Principles of Finance exam are distributed in the following way: Financial Statements and Planning—20%, Time Value of Money—20%, Working Capital Management—10%, Valuation and Characteristics of Stocks and Bonds—9%, Capital Budgeting—12%, Cost of Capital—11%, Risk and Return—11%, and International Financial Management—7%.

In addition to the breakdown of topics on a DSST exam, the fact sheet also lists recommended reference materials. If you do not own the recommended books, then check college bookstores. Avoid paying high prices for new textbooks by looking online for used textbooks. Don't panic if you are unable to locate a specific textbook listed on the fact sheet; the textbooks are merely recommendations. Instead, search for comparable books used in university courses on the specific subject. Current editions are ideal, and it is a good idea to use at least two references when studying for a DSST exam. Of course, the subject matter provided in this book will be a sufficient review for most test takers. However, if you need additional information, then it is a good idea to have some of the reference materials at your disposal when preparing for a DSST exam.

Fact sheets include other useful information in addition to a list of reference materials and topics. Each fact sheet includes subject-specific sample questions like those you will encounter on the DSST exam. The sample questions provide an idea of the types of questions you can expect on the exam. Test questions are multiple-choice with one correct answer and three incorrect choices.

The fact sheet also includes information about the number of credit hours ACE has recommended be awarded by colleges for a passing DSST exam score. However, you should keep in mind that not all universities and colleges adhere to the ACE recommendation for DSST credit hours. Some institutions require DSST exam scores higher than the minimum score recommended by ACE. Once you have acquired appropriate reference materials and you have the outline provided on the fact sheet, you are ready to start studying, which is where this book can help.

TEST DAY

After reviewing the material and taking practice tests, you are finally ready to take your DSST exam. Follow these tips for a successful test day experience.

1. **Arrive on time.** Not only is it courteous to arrive on time to the DSST testing facility, but it also allows plenty of time for you to take care of check-in procedures and settle into your surroundings.
2. **Bring identification.** DSST test facilities require that candidates bring a valid government-issued identification card with a current photo and signature. Acceptable forms of identification include a current driver's license, passport, military identification card, or state-issued identification card. Individuals who fail to bring proper identification to the DSST testing facility will not be allowed to take an exam.
3. **Bring the right supplies.** If your exam requires the use of a calculator, you may bring a calculator that meets the specifications. For paper-based exams, you may also bring No. 2 pencils with an eraser and black ballpoint pens. Regardless of the exam methodology, you are NOT allowed to bring reference or study materials, scratch paper, or electronics such as cell phones, personal handheld devices, cameras, alarm wrist watches, or tape recorders to the testing center.
4. **Take the test.** During the exam, take the time to read each question-and-answer option carefully. Eliminate the choices you know are incorrect to narrow the number of potential answers. If a question completely stumps you, take an educated guess and move on—remember that DSSTs are timed; you will have 2 hours to take the exam.

With the proper preparation, DSST exams will save you both time and money. So join the thousands of people who have already reaped the benefits of DSST exams and move closer than ever to your college degree.

PRINCIPLES OF FINANCE EXAM FACTS

The DSST® Principles of Finance exam consists of 100 multiple-choice questions that assess students for knowledge equivalent to that acquired in a Principles of Finance college course. The exam includes the following topics: Financial Statements and Planning, Time Value of Money, Working Capital Management, Valuation and Characteristics of Stocks and Bonds, Capital Budgeting, Cost of Capital, Risk and Return, and International Financial Management.

Area or Course Equivalent: Principles of Finance
Level: Lower-level baccalaureate
Amount of Credit: 3 Semester Hours
Minimum Score: 400
Source: : https://www.getcollegecredit.com/wp-content/assets/
factsheets/PrinciplesOfFinance.pdf

I. **Financial Statements and Planning – 20%**

   a. Fundamentals of financial statements (e.g., balance sheet, income statement, statement of cash flows, statement of owner equity)

   b. Ratio analysis (e.g., liquidity, solvency, market prospect, profitability, DuPont)

   c. Taxes (e.g., average vs. marginal tax rates, corporate tax rates)

II. **Time Value of Money – 20%**

   a. Present value (lump sum and annuity)

   b. Future value (lump sum and annuity)

   c. Annuity due vs. ordinary annuity

   d. Interest rate calculations (e.g. Equivalent Annual Rate [EAR], Annualized Percentage Rate [APR])

III. **Working Capital Management – 10%**

   a. Short-term sources of funds

   b. Management of short-term assets and liabilities (e.g., inventory, account receivables, accounts payable, short-term investments)

   c. Cash budget

IV. **Valuation and Characteristics of Stocks and Bonds – 9%**

   a. Bonds (e.g., debenture, sinking funds, coupon)

   b. Common stock and preferred stock (i.e., dividend)

V. Capital Budgeting – 12%

    a. Capital asset (e.g., building and equipment)

    b. Project cash flow forecasting and analysis (e.g., incremental, total, pro forma)

    c. Financial analysis tools (e.g., Net Present Value, Payback, Accounting Rate of Return [ARR], Internal Rate of Return [IRR])

    d. Break even and sensitivity analysis

VI. Cost of Capital – 11%

    a. Cost of Debt

    b. Cost of equity (e.g., common and preferred stock)

    c. Weighted average cost of capital

VII. Risk and Return – 11%

    a. Expected return on an asset and a portfolio

    b. Measures of risk (e.g., standard deviation, beta)

    c. Determinants of interest rates (e.g., real and nominal)

    d. Capital Asset Pricing Model (CAPM) and Security Market Line (SML) (e.g., beta and risk premium)

    e. Diversification (e.g., market risk, company specific risk, portfolio risk)

VIII. International Financial Management – 7%

    a. Impact of exchange rates on international financial markets

    b. Currency risk and political risk

    c. Tools (e.g., Spot vs. Forward, hedging)

Chapter 2

Principles of Finance Diagnostic Test

DIAGNOSTIC TEST ANSWER SHEET

1. Ⓐ Ⓑ Ⓒ Ⓓ
2. Ⓐ Ⓑ Ⓒ Ⓓ
3. Ⓐ Ⓑ Ⓒ Ⓓ
4. Ⓐ Ⓑ Ⓒ Ⓓ
5. Ⓐ Ⓑ Ⓒ Ⓓ
6. Ⓐ Ⓑ Ⓒ Ⓓ
7. Ⓐ Ⓑ Ⓒ Ⓓ

8. Ⓐ Ⓑ Ⓒ Ⓓ
9. Ⓐ Ⓑ Ⓒ Ⓓ
10. Ⓐ Ⓑ Ⓒ Ⓓ
11. Ⓐ Ⓑ Ⓒ Ⓓ
12. Ⓐ Ⓑ Ⓒ Ⓓ
13. Ⓐ Ⓑ Ⓒ Ⓓ
14. Ⓐ Ⓑ Ⓒ Ⓓ

15. Ⓐ Ⓑ Ⓒ Ⓓ
16. Ⓐ Ⓑ Ⓒ Ⓓ
17. Ⓐ Ⓑ Ⓒ Ⓓ
18. Ⓐ Ⓑ Ⓒ Ⓓ
19. Ⓐ Ⓑ Ⓒ Ⓓ
20. Ⓐ Ⓑ Ⓒ Ⓓ

PRINCIPLES OF FINANCE DIAGNOSTIC TEST
24 minutes—20 questions

Directions: Carefully read each of the following 20 questions. Choose the best answer to each question and fill in the corresponding circle on the answer sheet. The Answer Key and Explanations can be found following this Diagnostic Test.

---

1. Which of the following equities is considered a "hybrid" form of capital?

    A. Common stock
    B. Additional-paid-in capital
    C. Debenture
    D. Preferred stock

2. What is the future value of a $10,000 per year annuity that continues for 6 years at an annual interest rate of 8%? (Assume an ordinary annuity.)

    A. More than $60,000 but not more than $70,000
    B. More than $70,000 but not more than $80,000
    C. More than $80,000 but not more than $90,000
    D. More than $90,000 but not more than $100,000

3. Which of the following formulas calculates net working capital?

    A. Current assets minus total liabilities
    B. Total assets minus total liabilities
    C. Total assets minus current liabilities
    D. Current assets minus current liabilities

4. If a company's target profit is $100,000, its fixed costs are $600,000, the selling price of its product is $30, and its variable cost per unit is $10, what is its break-even point in units?

    A. 20,000
    B. 30,000
    C. 35,000
    D. 60,000

5. Which of the following ratios could be used to give an indication of liquidity?

A. Inventory turnover
B. Gross profit margin
C. Quick ratio
D. Net profit margin

6. Which of the following is NOT a capital asset investment?

A. A company spends $50,000 on new brakes for its large fleet of delivery vehicles.
B. A company purchases a building for a new headquarters.
C. A company spends $100,000 to replace three engines in its service vehicles.
D. A company acquires 25 forklift trucks for its factory.

7. What is the future value of $500,000 to be received in 5 years if the annual interest rate is 10%?

A. Over $600,000 but not more than $700,000
B. Over $700,000 but not more than $800,000
C. Over $800,000 but not more than $900,000
D. Over $900,000 but not more than $1,000,000

8. A _____ currency contract is an agreement to exchange one country's currency for another country's currency at a fixed price at a specified date in the future.

A. spot
B. forward
C. swap
D. prime

9. What is the present value of a 10-year annuity of $15,000 if the relevant annual interest rate is 5%? (Assume an ordinary annuity.)

A. Over $100,000 but not more than $110,000
B. Over $110,000 but not more than $120,000
C. Over $120,000 but not more than $130,000
D. Over $130,000 but not more than $140,000

10. It is estimated that a potential investment has the following possible returns and associated probabilities:

Rate of return 20% with a probability of 70%
Rate of return (10%) with a probability of 30%

What is the expected return?

A. 20%
B. 11%
C. 10%
D. (10%)

11. A company owes $100,000 of income taxes on net income of $400,000 to date and $2,000 on the next $10,000 that it earns. It is anticipated that in the next accounting period, corporate income tax rates will fall as a result of legislative action to a flat tax of 15%. What is the company's current marginal income tax rate?

A. 15%
B. 20%
C. 21%
D. 25%

12. A bank charges a prime rate of 8% but charges the XYZ Corporation 12% annual interest on a 5-year loan while inflation is running at an annual rate of 3%. What is the real rate of interest charged to XYZ Corporation?

A. 5%
B. 8%
C. 9%
D. 12%

13. What does a bond sinking fund accomplish?

    A. It provides a source of cash for the corporation to pay the bondholders upon maturity of the bond.

    B. It provides a source of cash for the corporation to purchase bonds as part of its marketable securities portfolio.

    C. It provides a source of cash for capital asset projects.

    D. It provides a source of cash to pay current liabilities during the life of a bond.

14. Which of the following is a spontaneous form of financing?

    A. Accounts payable

    B. Short-term bank loan

    C. Corporate bond

    D. Common stock

15. Which of the following capital budgeting methods do NOT account for the time value of money?

    I. Net Present Value (NPV)

    II. Payback period

    III. Accounting Rate of Return (ARR)

    IV. Internal Rate of Return (IRR)

    A. II only

    B. II and III only

    C. I and IV only

    D. III and IV only

16. Which of the following formulas would help you estimate the cost of preferred stock?

    A. Interest rate $\times$ (1 − tax rate)

    B. Dividend / price + growth rate of dividend

    C. Divided / price

    D. Dividend / price $\times$ (1 − tax rate)

17. Jimmy believes he can earn an 11% annual rate of return on his investment account. He has performed time value of money calculations and decides to invest $6,416 today in order for his investment account to be worth enough make a down payment on a home in 6 years. Which of the following is true?

    I. Jimmy could calculate the amount he will have for the down payment with this formula: $FV_n \times 1 / (1 + i)^n$

    II. Jimmy could calculate the down payment amount with this formula: $P(1 + i)^n$

    III. Jimmy should use the future value of an annuity formula to calculate the amount of the down payment.

    IV. The amount of the down payment will be about $12,000.

    A. I only
    B. I and II
    C. II and III
    D. II and IV

18. For which of the following forms of financing must the cost of capital be adjusted to account for tax deductibility?

    A. Retained earnings
    B. Bonds
    C. Preferred stock
    D. Common stock

19. Fees earned by a bank for the most recent accounting period would be revealed on which of the following financial statements?

    A. Income statement
    B. Balance sheet
    C. Statement of owners' equity
    D. Statement of cash flows

20. Which of the following financial statements would reveal the cost of a company's trademarks, the pension obligation to its employees and retirees, and the amount of capital contributed by its owners?

    A. Income statement
    B. Balance sheet
    C. Statement of owners' equity
    D. Statement of cash flows

ANSWER KEY AND EXPLANATIONS

1. D	**5.** C	**9.** B	**13.** B	**17.** D
2. B	**6.** A	**10.** B	**14.** A	**18.** B
3. D	**7.** C	**11.** B	**15.** B	**19.** A
4. B	**8.** B	**12.** C	**16.** C	**20.** B

1. **The correct answer is D.** Preferred stock is considered a "hybrid" form of capital, as it has the fixed cost (dividend) that is similar to the interest on a bond while it is technically a form of equity like common stock. Choices A and B are both types of common stock equity, which is pure ownership and not a hybrid with any of the characteristics of debt financing. A debenture (choice C) is just another term for bond, which is purely a debt security and not a hybrid of debt and equity.

2. **The correct answer is B.** Ordinary annuity means that the cash flows are assumed to occur at the end of each year. When calculated using the FV function in Microsoft Excel or a financial calculator, the future value of a $10,000 per year annuity that continues for 6 years at an annual interest rate of 8% is $73,359.29. When calculated using a time value of money table for the future value of a $1 ordinary annuity, the future value is about $73,360. The discrepancy in the answer is due to the table utilizing rounded factors.

3. **The correct answer is D.** The formula for net working capital is:

   Current Assets − Current Liabilities = Net Working Capital

4. **The correct answer is B.** The break-even point can be found by dividing the fixed costs by the difference between the selling price and the variable cost per unit. The difference between the selling price and the variable cost per unit is the contribution margin, which in this case is $20. The break-even point is 30,000 units ($600,000 / ($30 − $10) = 30,000 units. Choice A is incorrect because 20,000 is the result of erroneously dividing the selling price into the fixed costs. Choice C is incorrect because 35,000 units would be the volume needed to achieve a target profit of $100,000. Choice D is incorrect as 60,000 is the result of erroneously dividing the variable costs per unit into the fixed costs.

5. The correct answer is C. Quick ratio is calculated by dividing the most liquid of assets by the current liabilities to show the number of times the current liabilities could be paid from the most liquid assets. Inventory turnover (choice A) is more of an indication of how quickly the form sells its inventory. Gross profit margin (choice B) and net profit margins (choice D) are indications of profitability.

6. The correct answer is A. Expenditures for normal repairs and maintenance are not capital asset acquisitions. An expenditure must extend the useful life of the asset to be considered a capital asset investment as opposed to an operating expense. The purchase of a building (choice B), an expenditure to extend the useful life of a capital asset (choice C), and the acquisition of equipment (choice D) are all examples of capital asset investment.

7. The correct answer is C. The future value of $500,000 invested for 5 years at an annual rate of return of 10% is $805,255, using Microsoft Excel or a financial calculator and about $805,500 if you use a time value of money future value of $1 table. Remember, there will be a discrepancy in the exact answer, depending upon which tool you use to calculate the value.

8. The correct answer is B. A forward currency contract (also called futures contract) is an agreement to exchange one currency for another at a specified date in the future at a price (exchange rate) that is fixed on the purchase date. A spot rate (choice A) is the rate that would be paid now (in the present) for a foreign currency. A currency swap (choice C) is an agreement in which two parties exchange the principal amount of a loan and the interest in one currency for the principal and interest in another currency with rates at the spot rates. There is no such thing as a prime currency contract (choice D).

9. The correct answer is B. The present value of the annuity is $115,826.02 when calculated using Microsoft Excel's PV function or a financial calculator. It is about $115,830 when calculated using a time value of money table for the present value of a $1 ordinary annuity. Keep in mind that when using a table, the time value of money factors are rounded, and therefore, there will be a discrepancy in the exact answers, depending upon which tool you use to calculate the value.

10. **The correct answer is B.** The expected return is found by multiplying the possible returns by their associated probabilities and summing the results:

$$(20\% \times 0.7 + (10\%) \times 0.3) = 11\%$$

Choices A and D represent one, not both possible returns. Choice C is the result of equal weights (equal probabilities 50/50).

11. **The correct answer is B.** The marginal tax rate is the income tax rate paid on the next dollar earned. Based on the information given in the question, the marginal tax rate is 20%, computed as $2,000 / $10,000 = 20%. Choice A represents the flat tax rate expected for next year, which could possibly be next year's marginal and average tax rate. Choice C is incorrect as there is no evidence in the question that the company is paying a flat tax or marginal tax rate of 21%. Choice D represents the average tax rate paid to date.

12. **The correct answer is C.** The real rate of interest is the nominal rate (the amount charged) less the inflation rate, which for XYZ Corporation is 9% (computed as 12% – 3% inflation rate = 9%). Choice A represents the real rate of interest on prime rate loans. Choice B is the prime rate, which is the nominal rate charged to the bank's best customers. Choice D is represents the nominal rate charged to XYZ Corporation.

13. **The correct answer is B.** A bond sinking fund provides a source of cash for the corporation to purchase bonds as part of its marketable securities portfolio.

14. **The correct answer is A.** Spontaneous financing happens automatically as a firm grows. Accounts payable will increase as more goods and services are purchased on credit from vendors as the company gears up for more sales. Short-term bank loans (choice B), corporate bonds (choice C), and common stock (choice D) are forms of financing that must be arranged in advance.

15. **The correct answer is B.** The payback period (option II) and the accounting rate of return (option III) methods do not involve the discount of cash flows, while NPV and IRR do.

16. **The correct answer is C.** The cost of preferred stock is estimated by dividing its dividend per share by its share price. Choice A represents an estimate of the cost of debt. Choice B represents an estimated per share value of a stock with a growing dividend, and since preferred stock dividends are fixed (not anticipated to grow), it would only be relevant to the cost of common stock. Choice D is incorrect because a dividend payment is not tax deductible, and therefore no adjustment is needed.

17. **The correct answer is D.** An amount to be received in the future is a future value, and the amount the account will grow to is $12,000 (via the formula given in Option II). Thus, options II and IV are true. The formula given in option I is the calculation of a present value, so this option does not hold true. Option III is also not true because the future value of an annuity is not the arrangement described. This arrangement is a lump sum, not a stream of equal cash flows.

18. **The correct answer is B.** Bonds pay interest, and since interest is a tax-deductible expense for a business, the true cost of bonds is found by multiplying interest (or the interest rate) by (1 – tax rate). Retained earnings (choice A), preferred stock (choice C), and common stock (choice D) costs are partially related to dividends, which are not a tax-deductible business expense. Therefore, once you estimate the cost of capital for equity items, no adjustment downward is needed because of tax deductibility.

19. **The correct answer is A.** Fees earned by a bank are a type of revenue, and revenues are disclosed on the income statement. The balance sheet (choice B) does not reveal revenues—it shows assets, liabilities, and equity. The statement of owners' equity (choice C) shows the changes in equity that occurred during a particular period. The statement of cash flows (choice D) shows the changes in the cash account during the period.

20. **The correct answer is B.** The balance sheet shows the assets, liabilities, and equity accounts of a business. A company's trademark is an asset, its pension obligations are a type of liability, and the amount of capital contributed by the owners is equity. Income statements (choice A) show a business's revenues and expenses. The statement of owners' equity (choice C) shows the changes in equity that occurred during a particular period. The statement of cash flows (choice D) shows the changes in the cash account during the period.

DIAGNOSTIC TEST ASSESSMENT GRID

Now that you've completed the diagnostic test and read through the answer explanations, you can use your results to target your studying. Find the question numbers from the diagnostic test that you answered incorrectly and highlight or circle them below. Then focus extra attention on the sections dealing with those topics.

Principles of Finance		
Content Area	**Topic**	**Question #**
Financial Statements and Planning	• Fundamentals of financial statements • Ratio analysis • Taxes	5, 11, 19, 20
Time Value of Money	• Present value (lump sum and annuity) • Future value (lump sum and annuity) • Annuity due vs. ordinary annuity • Interest rate calculations	2, 7, 9, 17
Working Capital Management	• Short-term sources of funds • Management of short-term assets and liabilities • Cash Budget	3, 14
Valuation and Characteristics of Stocks and Bonds	• Bonds • Common stock and preferred stock	1, 13
Capital Budgeting	• Capital asset • Project cash flow forecasting and analysis • Financial analysis tools • Break even and sensitivity analysis	4, 6, 15
Cost of Capital	• Cost of debt • Cost of equity • Weighted average cost of capital	16, 18

Principles of Finance

Content Area	Topic	Question #
Risk and Return	• Expected return on an asset and a portfolio • Measures of risk • Determinants of interest rates • Capital Asset Pricing Model (CAPM) and Security Market Line (SML) • Diversification	10, 12
International Financial Management	• Impact of exchange rates on international financial markets • Currency risk and political risk • Tools	8

Chapter 3

Principles of Finance Subject Review

OVERVIEW

- Financial Statements and Planning
- Time Value of Money
- Working Capital Management
- Valuation and Characteristics of Stocks and Bonds
- Capital Budgeting
- Cost of Capital
- Risk and Return
- International Financial Management
- Summing It Up

FINANCIAL STATEMENTS AND PLANNING

Financial statements are the primary tools used to communicate and evaluate results of operations, financial position, and cash flow activity of a business. Summarizing results from past periods, the **income statement** and the **statement of cash flows** reveal revenues, expenses, and the sources and uses of cash, respectively, covering a specified period. A **balance sheet** shows the financial condition of the business, specifically the assets owned, the liabilities owed, and the equity of the owners as of a point in time.

Financial statements can also be prepared based on expectations and fore-casts. **Pro forma financial statements**, prepared based on expectations of future results, are tools of corporate financial planning. For example, if a CFO wants to see the effects of possible financing options on the financial position of the business she may prepare a set of pro forma balance sheets, income statements, and statements of cash flow that reflect educated guesses regarding what the future may bring. Pro forma financial statements are also part of the financial budget, a key output of the financial planning process.

Fundamentals of Financial Statements

Financial statements are prepared at the end of an accounting cycle, based on information from the company's **general ledger**—i.e., its collection of accounts. A focus of financial analysis, financial statements of large public corporations are a critical part of each 10-K, an annual report filed with the Securities and Exchange Commission that discloses financial performance and condition.

Income Statement

The key elements of an income statement are as follows:
- Revenues
- Expenses
- Gains
- Losses
- Net income (or net loss)

Revenues are amounts earned by a business from selling its products or by providing services during a specific period, such as a year. Revenues may include sales of products (sales); rendering of services (fees); and earnings from interest, dividends, lease income, and royalties. **Net sales** refer to the value of a company's sales of goods and services to its customers after accounting for any returns or discounts granted as a result of early payments.

Expenses are the costs an entity incurs for doing business in a specific period, including the cost of materials, supplies, labor, leases, and utilities. In addition, expenses relate to producing revenues for an entity. The matching principle of accounting requires that revenues of a period (such as a year) are matched against the expenses that were incurred (happened) during that same period. Typical expenses include the following:
- **Cost of sales:** Depending upon the type of business, this is also referred to as cost of goods, cost of products, cost of goods sold (COGS), and cost of services. For a manufacturer, cost of sales is the expense incurred for raw materials, labor, and manufacturing overhead used in the production of its goods. It is equal to the cost of goods manufactured adjusted for the change

in finished goods. For wholesalers and retailers, the cost of sales is essentially the purchase cost of merchandise used for resale. It is calculated as beginning inventory plus purchases minus ending inventory.

- **Selling, general, and administrative expenses:** Often referred to as SG&A, these expenses make up a company's **operational expenses**. General and administrative (G&A) expenses are incurred for the whole of the entity as opposed to some expenses (like selling and manufacturing) that are specific to parts of the entity. G&A expenses include accounting, legal, fees for services, officers' salaries, insurance, wages of office staff, supplies, and office occupancy costs (such as rent, utilities, etc.).
- **Selling expenses:** These expenses are incurred in selling or marketing. Examples include sales commissions, sales representatives' salaries, rent for the sales department, traveling expenses, advertising, selling department salaries and expenses, the cost of samples given to potential customers, and credit and collection costs.

A company's **gross profit** (also called **gross margin**) does more than simply represent the difference between net sales and the cost of sales. Gross profit provides the resources to cover the company's other expenses. Obviously, the greater and more stable a company's gross margin, the greater potential there is for positive bottom line (net income) results.

Gains are possible from a variety of events and activities. Gains are from peripheral or incidental transactions of an entity. An example of a gain is when a retailer sells a building and a gain in wealth (selling at a price higher than cost) occurs. Such an event would not be as a result of core business activities (such as the retail sale of merchandise). The sale of a building by a retailer of merchandise would be incidental to the everyday business. Other gains can result from investments in stock and bonds and other financial assets.

Losses are decreases in owners' equity from peripheral or incidental transactions of an entity. Examples are losses on the sale of investments and losses from lawsuits.

Net income, or the "bottom line" as it is often called, is the excess of all revenues and gains for a designated period over all expenses and losses of that period. A **net loss** is the excess of expenses and losses over revenues and gains for a designated period. The formula for net income (and the basic skeleton of the income statement) is as follows:

Revenues – Expenses + Gains – Losses = Net Income of (Net Loss)

Statement of Retained Earnings/
Statement of Stockholders' Equity

Retained earnings is a type of equity. It is often defined as the amount of net income remaining after dividends have been paid to shareholders. The **statement of retained earnings** shows the increases and decreases to retained earnings for the same period as the income statement. As retained earnings grow, so does the owners' interest in the business. The formula embedded in the statement of retained earnings is as follows:

Beginning Balance of Retained Earnings

\+ Net Income or – Net Loss – Dividends

\= Ending Balance of Retained Earnings

The ending balance of retained earnings is the same balance that will be reported on the balance sheet.

The **statement of stockholders' equity** can be prepared as an alternative to the statement of retained earnings. Showing the changes in retained earnings, the statement of stockholders' equity additionally reveals the changes in other equity accounts that occurred during the same period as the income statement. Those changes can include issuance of stock, acquisition of the company's own stock (treasury stock), and payment of stock dividends.

Treasury stock represents negative equity and is shown on both the statement of stockholder's equity and the balance sheet as a subtraction from equity. Corporations acquire their own stock (treasury stock) to award bonuses to executives, for stock options exercised by management, or to prop up earnings per share.

Balance Sheet

The **balance sheet** is a "snapshot" of a company's financial position at a particular point in time. A logical starting point for assessing a company's financial position, the balance sheet is a key report for users of financial statements to review and analyze. From the balance sheet, we can learn a great deal about liquidity, solvency, financial flexibility, risk, and the sources of funds for the assets of a company.

NOTE: The balance sheet is also known as a **statement of financial position**.

The balance sheet is a detailed presentation of the following accounting equation:

$$Assets = Liabilities + Equity$$

Assets are the resources owned by the business; they represent expectations of amounts to be realized by the business. Assets are initially valued at their cost. **Liabilities** are debts and other obligations that arise during the course of business operations and their values represent expected future financial sacrifices. **Equity** is the different between assets and liabilities:

$$Assets - Liabilities = Equity$$

Within those major balance sheet classifications there are sub-classifications. Assets are broken out into **current assets** and **noncurrent assets**. Liabilities use the same current and noncurrent arrangement while equity can be detailed out into a variety of accounts based on the type of company. For example, a corporation will have some variation of equity classifications—such as common stock, preferred stock (contributed capital), and retained earnings.

Assets are presented on the balance sheet in descending order of liquidity with the most liquid of assets followed by the less liquid assets. **Liquidity** is the ability of an asset to be converted into cash quickly and without any loss or discount. Here is a typical order of the assets on the balance sheet:

ASSETS

Current assets

Cash

Accounts receivable

Inventory

Noncurrent assets

Investments

Property, plant, and equipment

Intangible assets

Current assets are reasonably expected to be converted into cash or consumed by the entity (e.g., supplies) within one year and in the normal course of business operations. Current assets include cash and other monetary assets such as accounts receivable, inventory, marketable securities, and prepaid expenses (such as supplies and insurance premiums covering future periods). Cash is always listed first because it is the most liquid of all assets.

Noncurrent assets, also called **long-term assets**, are to be held by the entity for a period longer than one year. Noncurrent assets are those assets whose benefits are expected to be realized or consumed over more than one year or normal operating cycle.

Property, plant, and equipment are also called **operating assets** since they are used to create revenue from the operations. Operating assets are carried at their acquisition cost minus accumulated depreciation. **Depreciation** is the reduction in historical cost of an operating asset over its useful life (how long you believe it will provide benefits).

Intangible assets, such as patents and trademarks, are also listed at their cost, but their book value is reduced over time through a concept called **amortization**. Amortization refers to the periodic write off of the cost of intangible assets over their useful lives. Intangible assets have no physical substance but have value based on rights, privileges, or advantages belonging to the owner.

Liabilities are shown on the balance sheet in a manner similar to assets. Listed in an order of time to maturity, liabilities are arranged into current and noncurrent (or long-term) liabilities.

LIABILITIES

Current liabilities

> Account payable
>
> Taxes payable
>
> Salaries and wages payable
>
> Unearned revenues
>
> Other accruals

Long-term liabilities

> Notes payable (due in one or more years into the future)
>
> Bonds payable
>
> Mortgages payable
>
> Other long-term obligations (such as pensions)

Current liabilities are obligations that will be paid (liquidated) by utilizing current assets. **Payables** are a typical current liability including amounts owed to vendors for purchases of inventory and supplies, wages and salaries owed, rent, and taxes to be paid. The portion of long-term debt (a noncurrent liability) that is due in the current period is also classified as a current liability.

Noncurrent liabilities (also called **long-term liabilities**) are those obligations that do not qualify as current liabilities and include long-term notes and bonds, amounts owed as a result of long-term leases, and obligations as a result of pensions promised to employees.

Equity is the difference between total assets and total liabilities and is usually presented on the balance sheet in the following order:

1. Common stock (par value + additional paid-in-capital)
2. Preferred stock (par value + additional paid-in-capital)
3. Treasury Stock
4. Retained Earnings

TIP: Understanding the role of assets, liabilities, and equity is integral to building a solid financial foundation.

Statement of Cash Flows

The **statement of cash flows** reports the cash effects of a company's activities. It does this by classifying cash effects in three ways: (1) cash effects of operating activities, (2) investing, and (3) financing.

- **Cash Flows from Operating Activities:** Cash flows from operating activities is cash that flowed in and out from the everyday business operations. One way to show cash flow from operating activities is to adjust net income. The adjustments are necessary because the concept of net income (based on accrual accounting rules) and cash flow are not synonymous. Cash flows from operating activities include cash received from sales and fees, interest on loans and dividends on equity securities, and cash payments to suppliers for inventory and other goods and services and to employees for services (salaries and wages), taxes, and payments made to lenders for interest.

- **Cash Flows from Investing Activities:** Cash flows from investing activities reports the change in a firm's cash position from any gains (or losses) from investments (in the financial markets), changes in cash resulting from amounts spent on investments in capital assets such as plant and equipment; acquiring and disposing of debt or equity instruments; and acquiring and disposing of property, plant, and equipment.
- **Cash Flows from Financing Activities:** Cash flows from financing activities measures the flow of cash between the company and its owners and creditors such as banks, bondholders, and stockholders. The activities include obtaining resources from owners and providing them with a return on investment (dividends), a return of investment (treasury stock transactions), borrowing money from creditors, and repaying the amounts borrowed.

Ratio Analysis

When trying to understand a business, one approach is to study the financial statements. Some basic knowledge can be gained from examining financial statements, such as how large the company is (total assets), how profitable the firm has been (net income), and the amount of positive or negative cash flow generated (statement of cash flows). Additional conclusions and insights can be reached through financial statement analysis, including ratio analysis, providing a deeper dive into the numbers.

A **ratio** is one financial item divided by another with the result being a factor that can be interpreted in a number of ways. Interpretation of financial ratios is done by making comparisons against benchmarks and trends, thereby creating additional insights for decision makers, such as investors who can utilize market prospect ratios like the price/earnings ratio to estimate the value of a share of common stock.

Benchmarks include industry averages and internally generated data. **Trends** reveal improvement to financial condition over time. Financial ratio analysis provides messages that are not revealed simply by reading and studying the numbers on the pages of the financial statements. Ratios can be organized by categories—e.g., profitability, asset utilization, liquidity, and debt utilization—as the following sections of this chapter explain. Keep in mind that there are many other ratios than those explained here. This is a sampling of the many ratios that are utilized by financial analysts.

Profitability Ratios

Profitability ratios are used to assess a business' ability to generate earnings relative to its revenue, assets, and shareholders' equity. Like all ratios, profitability ratios are compared over time and against benchmarks such as the profitability ratios of competitors or industry averages. An example of a profitability ratio is gross profit margin, which is found by dividing gross profit by net sales. Remember, gross profit is the difference between net sales and cost of goods sold.

Profit margin, also called **net profit margin**, is calculated by dividing net income by net sales (net revenues.) Other profitability ratios include return on assets and return on equity.

Asset Utilization Ratios

Asset utilization ratios indicate how well management is managing or utilizing its assets. One example is the Accounts Receivable turnover—the number of times per year that a business collects its average receivable. It is calculated with the following formula:

Annual Credit Sales / Average Accounts Receivable

Average accounts receivable is found by adding the beginning and ending accounts receivable balances and dividing by 2.

Other asset utilization ratios include the average collection period, inventory turnover, fixed asset turnover, and total asset turnover.

Liquidity Ratios

Assets that are **liquid** are easily and quickly turned into cash. A related concept is **solvency**, a company's ability to meet its short-term obligations. Two common liquidity ratios are the **current ratio** and the **quick ratio**. The current ratio is calculated by dividing current assets by current liabilities, while the quick ratio, which is also called the acid test, is calculated as follows:

(Current Assets – Inventory) / Current Liabilities

Debt Utilization Ratios

Debt utilization ratios measure financial leverage—the degree to which a company finances its operations with debt. Examples include debt to total assets (total liabilities divided by total assets), times interest earned, and fixed charge coverage.

DuPont Model

Ratios can also be used in an integrated way to help understand a company's finances to see how various strategies can help a company improve its financial results. For example, the **DuPont model** for return on equity (ROE) is a way of "drilling down" into factors of producing a yield for investors. The model provides a focus on this formula:

Return on Equity = Net Profit Margin × Asset Turnover × Equity Multiplier

where:
- Net Profit Margin = Net Income / Revenue
- Asset Turnover = Sales / Average Total Assets
- Equity Multiplier = Average Total Assets / Average Shareholders' Equity

Therefore, financial managers of a company can "play" with the model to discuss strategies that can improve profitability (measured by the profit margin), to increase asset turnover and to acquire more asset value relative to equity investment.

Taxes

Income taxes are an expense of doing business and decision makers must consider the impact of income taxes on a variety of decisions. A corporation is a separate legal entity and a taxpayer. As it is mandatory that a corporation reports its taxable income to the federal government (i.e., the IRS), and in many states to the state revenue department, a corporation is liable for the income taxes owed on that income. Companies that do business overseas may also owe foreign income taxes. Income tax expense is reported on the company's income statement and any tax owed as of the date of the balance sheet is reported as income taxes payable, a current liability.

There is the potential that some of the earnings of a corporation will be taxed twice. Any income paid out to shareholders of the corporation in the form of dividends is included in the shareholder's taxable income and therefore, it can be said that there is double taxation of earnings—once paid at the corporate level and once paid by shareholders on dividends that they receive.

A company's **average tax rate** is found by dividing the tax liability by the company's taxable income. The company's **marginal tax rate** is the rate that the company will pay on the next dollar of earnings.

TIME VALUE OF MONEY

Many financial decisions cannot be made without utilizing time value of money concepts. The **time value of money** has been called the "math" of finance, and it recognizes that a dollar today is not worth the same as a dollar in the future. A dollar in hand today can be invested and earn interest, which makes its **future value** more than the value today (**present value**). Time value of money calculations are used when computing compounding of interest on a savings account, when calculating the annual rate of return on an equity mutual fund, when calculating a loan payment, and when evaluating the projected cash flows from a capital project.

Loan amortizations, lease payments, and bond interest rates are all related to the principles of the time value of money. Both future and present values are important inputs into financial decision making, both in personal financial planning and business finance.

Students usually utilize financial calculators, Microsoft Excel functions, or time value of money tables of interest factors to calculate time value money concepts. The two basic concepts of time value of money are present value and future value, and the two basic types of cash flows are single amounts (also called lump sums) and annuities.

TIP: The time value of money can be calculated using a financial calculator, Microsoft Excel, or by referencing the correct time value of money table. Experiment with all three methods. You are allowed to use a nonprogrammable calculator during the exam, but you will waste valuable time if you don't know how to use it to calculate the correct value.

Present Value

There are times when it is useful to convert a future dollar amount into its equivalent in today's dollars. **Present value** is the current dollar amount of a future dollar amount.

Single Amounts (Lump Sum)

The process of calculating the present value of a future amount is also called discounting. **Discounting** involves a mathematical way of extracting interest (rate of return) from a future amount to reduce it to today's dollars. It is also called **reverse compounding**. The formula for discounting a future amount is as follows:

$$PV = FV \times 1 / (1 + i)^n$$

Where:
- PV is the present value of some future amount
- FV is the future value at the end of period n
- i is the annual rate of interest (or rate of return)

For example, the present value of $5,000 received at the end of year 5, assuming an annual interest rate of 8 percent, is $3,403, calculated as follows:

$$PV = FV \times 1(1+i)^n$$
$$PV = \$5,000 \times 1(1+0.08)^5$$
$$\$3,403 = \$5,000 \times 0.6806$$

Rather than using the formula, it is much easier to use the PV function in Microsoft Excel, a financial calculator, or a time value of money table. If you use the time value of money table, you must find the present value interest factor (PVIF) for a single amount and for the appropriate interest rate and number of periods. In the above example, the PVIF is 0.6806, which can be found at the intersection of 8 percent and 5 years in a present value of $1 table.

$$PV = FV \times PVIF\ 8\%,\ 5\ \text{years}$$
$$\$3,403 = \$5,000 \times 0.6806$$

There are many applications of present value. For example, if you have as your personal goal to accumulate $100,000 in 5 years and can invest your money at an annual rate of return of 7 percent, you can compute how much you must invest today to reach your goal. As the numbers show below, you would need to invest a lump sum of $71,300 now to achieve the $100,000 goal.

$$PV = FV \times PVIF \ 7\%, \ 5 \text{ years}$$
$$PV = \$100,000 \times 0.7130$$
$$PV = \$71,300$$

Present value is also used to value a series of uneven future cash flows, as is the case with many investments such as commercial enterprises, equities, and real estate. For example, if an investment is expected to have the variable cash flows (different each year), the present value of the cash flows would be calculated as single amounts for each period.

Present Value of an Annuity

An **annuity** is a series of cash flows that are equal each period for a definite period of time. A good example of a practical use of the present value of an annuity is a loan. The present value (the balance) of a loan is the present value of its future payments. For example, if a loan arrangement calls for 20 annual payments of $1,000 with an annual interest rate of 8 percent, the loan balance (principal) would be $9,818.10. The Present Value Interest Factor for an Annuity (PVIFA) would be found in a PVIFA table at the intersection of 8% and 20 periods.

$$PVA = A \times PVIFA \ 8\%, \ 20 \text{ years}$$
$$PVA = \$1,000 \times 9.8181$$
$$\$9,818.10 = \$1,000 \times 9.8181$$

When financial institutions sell loans—such as fixed-rate car loans, home equity loans, and mortgages to other institutions—the PVA formula is used to discount the future loan payments at a prevailing market interest rate. There are many applications of the present value of an annuity.

Future Value

A **future value** is derived by **compounding**, which is when interest is earned on interest. For example, if you invest $100 for a year at 5%, at the end of the year the account is worth $105 ($100 + $5 of interest). At the end of year two, the account grows to $110.25 with the second year of interest amounting to $5.25. The extra twenty-five (25) cents of interest in year two is the result of interest earned on interest. Future values can be calculated based on single amounts (lump sums) or annuities.

Single Amount (Lump Sum)

Money can grow in value over time because of interest or other types of returns (e.g., dividends or price appreciation). A dollar received today is really worth more than a dollar received a year from now because of the ability to earn a rate of return. Practical applications of future value of a single amount include estimating the value of an investment on the day you retire or when a child starts school, the amount that a US savings bond will be worth in 10 years, and the estimated value of your home five years from now when you think you may relocate.

Compound interest (or **rate of return**) is a big part of future value. Remember, compounding is when interest is earned on top of interest. Since most people think of rates as a yearly percentage, many governments and US banking regulators require financial institutions to disclose a comparable yearly interest rate on deposits. A compounded interest rate may be referred to as **annual percentage rate (APR)**, **effective interest rate**, or **effective annual rate**.

The basic formula for future value of a single amount is as follows:

$$FV_n = PV \times (1 + i)^n$$

Where
- FV_n is the future value at the end of period n
- PV is the initial principal (or deposit or investment), also called present value
- i is the annual rate of interest (or rate of return)

For example, if you invest $1,000 for one year at 8 percent interest, the future value would be $1,080, calculated as follows:

$$\$1,080 = \$1,000 \times (1 + 0.08)$$

If you invested $1,000 for three years at the same 8 percent interest, the future value would be $1,259.71, calculated as follows:

$$\$1,259.71 = \$1,000 \times (1 + 0.08)^3$$

In this second scenario, where money is invested for three years, the power of compounding is evident. The total interest earned of $259.71 ($1,259.71 – $1,000) is the result of interest on top of interest. Note that the year 1 interest was only $80, but year 2 and year 3 interest ($86.40 and $93.31) are a bit more than $80, as the following table shows.

Years	Beginning-of-Year Value	Interest	End-of-Year Value
1	$1,000.00	$80.00	$1,080.00
2	$1,080.00	$86.40	$1,166.40
3	$1,166.40	$93.31	$1,259.71

Using a future value interest factor table, you can calculate the future value by using the future value interest factor (FVIF) found at the intersection of 8 percent and three years. That factor is 1.2597 (rounded).

$$FV_n = PV \times FVIF\ 8\%,\ 3\ \text{years}$$
$$FV = \$1,000 \times 1.2597$$
$$FV = \$1,259.70$$

Future Value of an Annuity

An **annuity** is a series of equal cash flows for a definite period of time. A fixed-rate home mortgage is an annuity. For example, if you borrow $100,000 for 30 years at 8 percent interest, the payment is about $774 per month for 360 months.

As an insurance company product, an annuity is a type of investment vehicle that provides a fixed (set unchanging amount) monthly income. There are many examples of annuities in the finance world, including retirement annuities, loan payments, and lottery payouts.

The **future value of an annuity (FVA)** is the future value of a stream of payments (annuity), assuming the payments are invested at a given rate of interest. It is calculated as follows:

$$FVA = \frac{A \times \left(1 + i^{n-1}\right)}{i}$$

Where:
- *FVA* is future value of an annuity
- *A* is the value of the individual payments in each compounding period
- *i* is the interest rate per period
- *n* is the number of periods

If you use the Future Value of an Annuity table, you must find the future value interest factor for an annuity (FVIFA), which is found at the intersection of the number of periods and the rate.

Here's the formula:

$$FVA = A \times FVIFA\ i, n$$

Where:
- *FVA* is future value of an annuity
- *A* is the value of the individual payments in each compounding period
- *i* is the interest rate per period
- *n* is the number of periods
- *FVIFA* is the future value interest factor for an annuity

For example, the future value of a five-year $1,000 annuity, assuming a 9 percent annual interest, is $5,984.70, computed as follows:

$$FVA = A \times FVIFA\ 9\%,\ 5$$
$$FVA = \$1,000 \times 5984.7$$
$$FVA = \$5,984.70$$

Therefore, if you invest $1,000 per year for five years at an annual interest rate of 9 percent, the investment will accumulate to $5,984.70 by the end of year 5.

You can see how the future value of an annuity would have practical uses. If a company is attempting to put aside funds for purposes such as future capital investment, a sinking fund to pay off a loan or a bond, or a pension fund for employees, the future value of an annuity or some derivative of it would be used. For example, assume that in 10 years a company wants to retire a $10,000,000 bond issue. Assuming an interest rate of 7 percent, it could put aside about $145,000 per year, calculated as follows:

$$\frac{FVA}{FVIFA\ 7\%,\ 10\ \text{years}} = A$$

$$\frac{\$2,000,000}{13.8164} = \$144,755.51$$

Annuity Due vs. Ordinary Annuity

An **annuity due** is a repeating payment (same amount each period) that is made at the beginning of each period, such as when a 3-year lease for an office requires that the monthly rental payment be made the first day of each month. An **ordinary annuity** is a repeating payment that is made at the end of each period. When using a financial calculator or Microsoft Excel to calculate the present or future values of annuities, you must specify whether the annuity is an annuity due or an ordinary annuity for the calculations to be accurate. Time value of money tables are labeled as annuity due or ordinary annuity tables.

Uneven Cash Flows (Present Value and Future Value)

There are times when the cash flow is a mixed stream—such as an income real estate investment (with rising rental income and depreciation and operating expenses that vary each period). To calculate the present or future value of a stream of unequal cash flows, you discount or compound cash flow values individually. For example, the following cash inflows occur on a prospective investment:

Period	Cash Flow
1	$1,000
2	$1,200
3	$1,500
4	$2,000

If you assume an interest rate of 9 percent, you would find the present value of these cash flows as follows (using the present value interest factors from a time value of money table for single amounts (lump sums)):

Period	Cash Flow	$PVIF_{9,n}$	Present Value
1	$1,000	× 0.9174	$917.40
2	$1,200	× 0.8417	$1,010.04
3	$1,500	× 0.7722	$1,158.30
4	$2,000	× 0.7084	$1,416.80
		Total	$4,502.54

Each cash flow is multiplied by the appropriate PVIF for the period. For example, the cash flow for period 1 is multiplied by the PVIF for 9 percent and year 1, the period 2 cash flow is multiplied by the PVIF for 9 percent and year 2, and so on. Then the discounted cash flows are totaled to derive the present value of the stream of unequal cash flows. If this example was a proposed investment upon which a potential investor wanted a 9 percent periodic (e.g., annual) rate of return, then the investor should pay no more than $4,502.34 for the investment. Keep in mind that these same calculations can be done using the PV function in Microsoft Excel or by utilizing a financial calculator.

A similar procedure is used to find the future value of a stream of unequal cash flows. In that case, each periodic cash flow is multiplied by the appropriate FVIF. Using the same numbers, here's what a future value version would look like:

Period	Cash Flow	FVIF$_{9\%}$	Present Value
1	$1,000	× 1.4116	$1,411.60
2	$1,200	× 1.2950	$1,554.00
3	$1,500	× 1.1881	$1,782.15
4	$2,000	× 1.0900	$2,180.00
		Total	$6,927.75

The total of $6,927.75 is the value of the unequal stream of cash flows at the end of year 4 (assuming the periods represent years). The future value includes $1,227.75 of interest that would accumulate period by period assuming a 9 percent periodic return.

Of course, the present value and future value calculations of unequal cash flows can be performed with a financial calculator or within Microsoft Excel using the future value (FV) function.

Interest Rates

Interest is the cost of borrowing. An interest rate is the charge by a lender (to a borrower) for the use of money and is based on a 12-month period; interest rates are quoted on an annual (12-month) basis.

For example, an interest rate on a 90-day loan of 8% means that the loan would cost 8% of the principal (amount borrowed) over the course of 12 months. Another way to look at interest rates is to think of savers and investors: the interest rate is what a saver or investor earns (over 12 months) when they "lend" their money (such as is the case with a savings account, certificate of deposit, treasury bill, or corporate bond).

The **term structure of interest rates**, also known as the **yield curve**, shows levels of interest rates—both short-term and long-term rates—at a particular point in time. A normal relationship between time to maturity and interest rates is upward sloping, meaning that long-term yields are higher than short-term yields. An inverted or downward sloping term structure of interest rates means that long-term yields are lower than short-term yields.

Interest rate levels, and therefore the yield curve, change daily to reflect the demand for money, conditions in both the money and capital markets, inflation expectations, and other developments in the economy.

Various interest rate concepts include the following:
- **Prime rate:** Interest rate charged by banks to their best corporate customers
- **Discount rate:** Interest rate charged by the Federal Reserve to commercial banks
- **Federal Funds rate:** Interest that commercial banks charge other commercial banks for very short-term loans (i.e., overnight loans)
- **London Inter-Bank Offered Rate (LIBOR):** Interest rate average calculated from estimates submitted by the leading banks in London

Interest rates are usually discussed as nominal annual rates, but to get a more accurate idea of the real cost or investment (savings) yield, effective annual rates and annualized percentage rates are calculated by bankers, investors, and financial analysts.

Effective Annual Interest Rate

The **effective annual interest rate (EAR)** is the rate that is earned or paid on an investment, loan, or other financial product as a result of compounding.

The EAR is found by using the EFFECT function in Microsoft Excel or with the following formula:

$$(1 + \text{rate} / \text{number of compounding periods in the year})^n - 1$$

For example, if an investment earns 12% (nominal annual rate) with monthly compounding, the EAR is 12.68%:

$$(1 + 0.12 / 12)^{12} - 1 = 12.68$$

Annualized Percentage Rate

The **Annual Percentage Rate (APR)** helps explain the cost of borrowing and is useful when comparison shopping for loans. APR quotes your cost as a percentage of the loan amount that you pay each year. For example, if your loan has an APR of 12 percent, you will pay $12 per $100 you borrow annually. All other things being equal, the loan with the lowest APR is typically the least expensive. Financial calculators and the RATE function in Microsoft Excel are useful tools for calculating APR.

WORKING CAPITAL MANAGEMENT

Liquidity is a company's ability to meet its short-term liabilities as they become due. **Working capital** is the dollar difference between current assets and current liabilities. **Net working capital** is calculated as follows:

Current Assets – Current Liabilities = Net Working Capital

Working capital needs special attention and must be managed carefully. Too little working capital in a company runs the risk of not being able to meet obligations (pay bills). Too much capital tied up in working capital could mean that assets are not being employed productively. There is an **opportunity cost** of having too much cash, slow-paying receivables, and excess inventory.

Accounts receivable must be collected in a timely manner, inventory should be turned over quickly, and obligations such as accounts payable should be paid in timely manner to take advantage of discounts and to maintain a solid credit history.

Short-Term Sources of Funds

Short-term sources of funds include all current liabilities, including payables, accruals, and short-term bank loans. Payables and accruals are **spontaneous financing**, arising out of day-to-day operations, thereby providing liabilities almost automatically as business volume increases. Current assets, such as accounts receivable and inventory, can also be used to generate funds. For example, factoring occurs when a company sells its accounts receivable (i.e., invoices) to a third party, such as a bank (called a **factor**), at a discount.

Some bank loans require the borrower to keep a certain percentage of the loan amount of a minimum dollar balance on deposit at the bank. Such an arrangement is called a **compensating balance requirement**—a stipulation that adds to the true cost of the loan. For example, a loan agreement that charges 10% interest but requires that 20% of the loan amount be kept on deposit at the bank really costs the borrower 12.5% (12.5% = 10% / (100 − 20%)).

Management of Short-Term Assets and Liabilities

The **cash cycle** is the time period between when a business pays cash to its suppliers for its inventory and when it receives cash collections from customers. Receivables must be collected in a timely manner, inventory must be at optimal levels but also turned over (sold) quickly, and payables must be paid on time.

Receivables are amounts owed to the entity and can take two basic forms: **accounts receivable** and **notes receivable**. If the receivable arises from the sale of goods or services, it is an account receivable. Accounts receivable can be a very significant asset for companies that extend credit to their customers. Credit managers make their living on their ability to manage accounts receivable. They evaluate the **5Cs**: character, capacity, capital of the customer, collateral, and the economic conditions to decide whether credit should be extended to a customer.

Although accounts receivable is recorded when a sale is made and is initially entered into the books of the company at a value equal to the sale, the principal valuation factor is an estimation of the uncollectible accounts. The book value is the **net realizable value**, or the net recoverable amount of receivables. It is the total amount owed minus the estimated uncollectible amount.

Inventory consists of tangible personal property that is held for sale in the ordinary course of business. It can be composed of finished goods—items that are immediately available for sale—or those in various stages of production (also called **work-in-progress**). For example, in a manufacturing company, inventory can consist of raw materials, parts, work in progress, and finished goods. Inventory carries costs behind its historical costs (cost to produce it or acquire it). For example, there are costs related to storing inventory, spoilage costs, and obsolescence costs that occur as inventory ages.

Accounts payable is the money owed suppliers from the purchase of goods and services. Often, the credit terms on such debts allow for a discount to be taken for early payment. For example, credit terms of 2/10 net 30 on a payable means that if you make your payment by the 10th day after your purchase, you can take a 2% discount. Otherwise the full amount is owed (due) in 30 days (30 days from the invoice date).

Commercial paper is another short-term financing option for large corporations. Rather than use traditional bank loans, corporations float (sell) unsecured, short-term debt instruments to finance inventories and meet short-term liabilities. Maturities on commercial paper are rarely longer than 270 days, and the "paper" is usually issued at a discount from face value, reflecting prevailing market interest rates.

Cash Budget

A **budget** is a planning and control tool. The process of defining company goals, strategizing to achieve those goals, and budgeting for success is the essence of financial planning. As plans are executed, budgets are prepared with a comparison to actual results and the calculation of variances. A **variance** is the difference between the budgeted amount and the actual amount. To close the control loop, managers must explain why a variance exists. For example, if sales were budgeted at $1,100,000 but were only $900,000, the $200,000 unfavorable variance would prompt the question, "Why didn't we hit our budgeted sales figure?"

The **operating budget** is a collection of budgets including those for revenues (sales); cash needs; production, such as budgets for materials, labor, and overhead in manufacturing companies; selling and administrative expenses; and purchases. Operating budgets and capital budgets "feed" the preparation of the **pro forma financial statements**. The pro forma income statement is used to estimate whether expected profits will provide an accepted return to investors and if projected ratios, when compared to benchmarks, indicate acceptable levels of efficiency and effectiveness of operations. The pro forma balance sheet shows what the expected financial condition will be at some future point, such as a year from now.

TIP: There is a specific order for which budgets must be prepared because some information is linked—i.e., dependent upon information found in other budgets. For example, a cash budget is prepared *after* the operating budgets and the capital expenditures budget are prepared.

A cash budget is an important part of the operating budget. Cash flow is the life blood of a company, and a **cash budget** shows the projected cash inflows and outflows during a future period. The basic formula for a cash budget is as follows:

Beginning Cash Balance + Cash Inflows – Cash Outflows – Minimum Cash Balance = Surplus or Deficit

Managers use cash budgets as a planning tool for cash needs, short-term borrowings, and other planned sources of funds. The budgets are used to devise strategies to legitimately slow down payments and speed up collection of accounts receivable. Management usually likes to set a **minimum cash balance** in the budget and to maintain that balance during times of deficits, bank borrowing (such as a draw on a line of credit) may be necessary.

VALUATION AND CHARACTERISTICS OF STOCKS AND BONDS

Corporations issue shares of stock and bond certificates in return for cash from creditors (bondholders) and owners (shareholders). Bonds and stocks are components of a company's capital structure, and each carries its own cost. Investors (bondholders and stockholders) seek rates of return (investment yields) from the risk they take when investing in these securities.

Financial managers and investors must understand the capital structure of a corporation, by learning the attributes, the costs associated with each type of capital, and valuation principles of both stocks and bonds.

Bonds

A **bond** is a debt security similar to a long-term bank loan. When you purchase a bond, you are lending money to a government, municipality, federal agency, or corporation known as the **bond issuer**. In return for the loan, the bond issuer promises to pay a specified rate of interest to the investor during the life of the bond and to repay the face value of the bond (the principal) when it "matures" (comes due). Most debentures are **unsecured**, meaning that only the future cash flows generated by the issuing company stand behind the bond. A **secured bond** would be backed by an asset of some type that would be available to generate cash in the worst-case scenario of a default.

....

Note: Bonds are also called **debentures**. Most debentures are unsecured, however, secured bonds that are backed by an assets do exist.

....

Many entities issue bonds to raise funds to finance their long-life projects and long-term assets. In the United States, the federal government is a big issuer of bonds. States and municipalities also issue bonds to provide funds for all types of programs, to help run school districts and fire and police departments, and to build and maintain the infrastructure of a government.

Corporations, both for profit and nonprofit, also issue bonds. Some are extremely safe investments, such as the bonds of public utilities; other bond investments are riskier, such as those issued by industrial and transportation companies that might have revenues and earnings that are cyclical or have experienced the ups and downs of free enterprise.

Although anyone with enough money can buy a bond, institutional investors (banks, pension funds, and insurance companies) make up between 90–95 percent of the holders of bonds. Bond choices for investors range from the highest credit quality US Treasury securities (which are backed by the full faith and credit of the US government) to bonds that are below investment grade and considered speculative (known as **junk bonds**).

As is the case with any publicly traded financial asset, when a bond is issued, the issuer is responsible for providing details as to its financial soundness and creditworthiness. This information is contained in a document known as an offering document or **prospectus**.

Rating agencies assign ratings to many bonds when they are issued and monitor developments during the bond's lifetime. Financial services companies, securities firms, and banks also maintain research staffs that monitor the safety of bonds floated by the various corporations, governments, and other issuers.

Grading by debt rating agencies, such as Standard & Poor's (S&P), provides classifications so that potential investors can determine the investment worthiness of a bond. The S&P ratings are as follows:

Rating	Cash Flow
AAA	Excellent
AA	Very Good
A	Good
BBB	Adequate
CCC	Currently vulnerable to nonpayment
C	Highly vulnerable to nonpayment
D	In default

Any bond that carries a rating lower than BBB is said to be of speculative grade, or a junk bond. Junk bonds are risky investments that offer the possibilities of high yields but are also high risk—a perfect illustration of the risk/return trade-off of investing. Junk bonds are rated C or D by S&P. The balance between the desire to minimize risk and the highest possible returns of an investment must be considered when choosing investments (such as junk bonds) for a portfolio. Investors interested in risky but potentially high-yielding bonds must consider how much risk they are willing to accept.

Bond Fundamentals

Like any financial instrument, bonds have their own vocabulary and fundamentals. Before we review the fundamentals, let's take a look at a list of the types of bonds available.

- **Treasury bonds:** issued by the US government's treasury department
- **Other US government bonds:** issued by various agencies of the US federal government
- **Investment-grade corporate bonds:** high-quality (relatively safe) bonds issued by corporations

- **High-yield corporate bonds:** low-quality bonds, also known as junk bonds, issued by corporations
- **Mortgage-backed bonds:** bonds issued by corporations and backed by collateral like as real estate or equipment
- **Municipal bonds:** bonds issued by local, city, and state governments

There are three key fundamental concepts associated with bonds:

1. Interest rate
2. Term
3. Principal or maturity value

Bonds pay interest that is often fixed but there are also bond issues that pay a variable (floating) rate, or bonds that pay interest at maturity, rather than at specified periodic dates. Most bonds carry an interest rate that stays fixed until maturity and is a percentage of the face value (principal) amount of the bond. The typical face value of a bond is $1,000. However, there are some exceptions to that rule. Some states or municipalities issue mini bonds with face values as small as $100. There are also very small denominations of US savings bonds with face values as small as $50.

Typically, investors receive interest payments semiannually. For example, a $1,000 bond with a 7 percent interest rate will pay investors $70 a year, in payments of $35 every six months. If the investor is a corporation, the interest expense of a bond is tax deductible. This creates a tax shield, computed as follows:

Corporate Tax Shield =
Income Tax Rate of the Bond Issuer × Interest Expense of the Bond

A bond's **maturity** refers to the specific future date on which the investor's principal will be repaid. In other words, when a bond matures, investors are promised the full face amount of the bond—usually $1,000 per bond. Bonds are referred to by their maturities, which generally range from one day up to 30 years. In some rare cases, bonds have been issued for terms of up to 100 years. **Short-term notes/bonds** typically have maturities of up to 5 years, **intermediate notes/bonds** have maturities of 5–12 years, and **long-term bonds** have maturities of 12 or more years.

While the maturity period is a good expectation as to how long the bond will be outstanding, certain bonds have features that can substantially change the expected life of the bond. For example, some bonds have **redemption**, or **"call" provisions** that allow the bond issuer to repay the investors' principal at a specified date before maturity.

Bonds are "called" when prevailing interest rates have dropped significantly—an opportunity for the bond issuer to refinance the bond issue at a lower interest rate and therefore save significant expense. Bonds with a call provision usually have a higher annual return to compensate for the risk that the bonds might be called early.

As part of the **bond indenture** (i.e., the **bond contract**), some corporate issuers of bonds are required to set up a **sinking fund**, which is a fund into which money is deposited for the repayment of a bond. The existence of a sinking fund lowers the investment risk of the bond. Bond indentures can also detail other stipulations, such as a call provision, which grants the bond issuer the right to buy back all or some of a bond issue prior to the maturity date.

As a general rule, bonds are considered a lower-risk investment because of their predictable cash flows. However, not all bonds carry the same level of risks. Therefore, each bond investment should be analyzed carefully. The risks inherent in bonds include the following:

- **Interest rate risk:** the risk that interest rates will change and affect the price of a bond; generally, the longer the maturity, the greater the degree of interest rate risk
- **Default risk (also called business risk):** the risk that the bond issuer will fail to pay specified interest payments or principal at the promised time
- **Purchasing power risk (also called inflation risk):** the risk that you will lose value because of a loss of purchasing power due to inflation
- **Reinvestment rate risk:** the risk that interest rates will change and affect the rate that you earn on the reinvestment of your interest receipts
- **Liquidity risk:** the risk that you will be unable to find a buyer for the bond if you want to sell before the maturity date
- **Exchange rate risk:** the risk that exists in bonds that are denominated in a currency other than your own
- **Event risk:** the risk that the issuing firm may experience an event that can affect price of bond
- **Call risk:** the risk that a bond may be called by the issuer prior to maturity

How to Value a Bond

The value of a bond is the present value of the expected cash flows from the bond, discounted at the required rate of return. Let's use a simple example of a bond that pays annual interest.

Although most bonds pay semi-annual interest, for simplicity sake, we will present an annual interest example to illustrate how the bond valuation model works.

Assume that a particular bond pays $100 interest per year, has a maturity value of $1,000, and will mature in 10 years. Additionally, assume that the investors required rate of return on such an investment is 12 percent. The following are the cash flows (all inflows) associated with the bond investment:

Years	Cash Flow
1	$100
2	$100
3	$100
4	$100
5	$100
6	$100
7	$100
8	$100
9	$100
10	$1,100

In years 1 through 9, the cash flows are the interest payments, while in the last year (year 10) the $1,100 represents the last year of interest ($100) plus the maturity value ($1,000).

To estimate the value of this bond, you must discount the cash flows using the time value of money calculations. You can find the present value of an annuity (10 years, $100) and the present value of a single amount (year 10 maturity value of $1,000) and sum them.

You value the annuity by multiplying the $100 interest payment by 5.6502, which is the present value interest factor for an annuity, assuming 10 years and 12 percent interest. That means the interest payments are presently worth $565.02. Then you must find the present value of the maturity payment using the PVIF 10 years, 12% ($1,000 × 0.322 = $322). Add the two present values ($565.02 + $322) to derive a bond value of $587.02 (off by one cent due to rounding).

A **zero coupon** bond is an arrangement whereby the investor buys the bond at a significant discount and the bond does not pay periodic interest. A **discounted bond** means that the bond is selling for a value less than its face value (maturity value). For example, a 10-year zero coupon bond that has a yield to maturity of 5.24% and a face value of $1,000 would be purchased for about $600, which is $400 below (discount) its face value. The investor earns the yield by holding the bond till its maturity (redemption) date.

Bond Value Behavior

Why would a bond value be less than the maturity or face value of $1,000? The answer is that when the investor's required return is greater than the bond's stated interest rate (also called its **coupon rate**), the bond value is *discounted* to compensate the investor. The reverse is true when the investor's required return is less than the bond's coupon rate. In that case, the bond will sell (be valued) at a *premium*—an amount greater than the face value. As interest rates in the market rise, bond values fall, and when market rates fall, bond values rise. Interest rate risk is an inverse relationship between interest rate movements and bond value movements—a relationship all bondholders must understand.

Yield to Maturity

Whenever the required return by bond investors is different from the coupon rate, the yield to maturity becomes the key metric to follow. The **yield to maturity (YTM)** is the rate of return that investors earn if they buy the bond at a specific price and hold it to maturity. The YTM assumes that the bond issuer makes all promised interest payments and pays the maturity value to the investor on the promised maturity date.

Finding the YTM of a bond is easy with a financial calculator or with Microsoft Excel. The function IRR (internal rate of return) in Microsoft Excel uses algorithms to find the rate that will discount the bond's cash flows (interest payments and maturity value) so that they exactly equal the bond's current market value. Without the aid of a financial calculator or Microsoft Excel, the process of calculating the YTM is time-consuming. It is a process of trial and error, a search for the interest rate that will discount the future cash flows to exactly equal the bond's purchase value.

Common Stock

Stock (common and preferred) is a form of equity in a corporation. Common stock is a truer form of ownership, while preferred stock is more of a hybrid form.

The true owners of a corporation are the common stockholders who have a **residual claim** to the assets. That means they will receive what is left (residual) in the event that the business is liquidated—i.e., assets sold and liabilities paid. However, as a common stockholder, there is no assurance of income (dividends), capital gain, or a return of investment. The only real assurances are that the common stockholders will not lose more than they invest (limited liability) and that they will have a voice, through their votes for directors, in the management and direction of the entity. The common stockholders are the owners of the firm and have the right to vote on important matters to the firm, such as the election of the board of directors, major mergers, and acquisitions.

Common stock when initially sold by a corporation is offered as an **initial public offering (IPO)**. IPOs happen in the **primary market** in which investors purchase the stock for cash from the issuing corporation. Once the shares are outstanding, the price per share is set by the **secondary market**—that is, the stock exchanges where shares are traded daily between investors.

Common stockholders look for two types of income: **dividends** and **capital gains**. However, neither type of wealth is a sure thing. To pay dividends, a corporation must have enough profit and cash. The board of directors will examine both the amount of retained earnings and the liquidity of the entity before declaring a dividend. The value of a share of common stock is a function of potential dividends and potential capital gains. But the key word is potential—common stock value is based on potential, if not speculative, future cash flows.

How to Value Common Stock

Investors rarely have to estimate the value of a share of common stock because the market does that. The market is made up of buyers and sellers of all shapes and sizes—from individuals to security analysts to large institutions. This market takes into account all the available information about the company and assesses risk to determine whether a particular share of stock is a good buy.

The **constant-growth formula**, also known as the **Gordon Growth Formula**, assumes that a company grows at a constant rate forever. A constant-growth stock's dividends are expected to grow at a constant rate in the foreseeable future. Certainly, many common stocks will not have constant growth of dividends and so the constant-growth model is nothing more than a starting point of value estimation. The formula is as follows:

$$P = \frac{D}{Ks - g}$$

Where:

- P is the estimate price (value per share)
- D is the next dividend
- K_s expected is rate of return
- g is growth rate

For example, if the dividend is $10 per share, with an investor's expected return of 7% and a dividend growth rate of 3%, the value (P) would be $250.

Another method for estimating value of common stock is the **price/earnings model**. The price/earnings model is especially useful when a company's stock is not traded publicly, and no market price exists. To figure the price/earnings ratio, follow these steps:

1. Determine the P/E ratio for the industry.
2. Calculate the earnings per share (EPS) of the company.
3. Multiply the P/E of the industry times the EPS of the company.

For example, Acme Inc. is in an industry in which the average price/earnings ratio is 12. Acme's latest earnings per share were $7.00. An estimated value for a share of its common stock is $84 ($7 × 12).

Book value per share is not really a valuation technique, but it can be a consideration when trying to determine a market value because it reflects the residual amount per share if the assets were sold for their accounting value (what they are listed at on the balance).

Most stocks sell at a price above book value, but there are times when a stock could be selling below its book value, especially if investors believe the assets are overvalued or that the assets are understated. Book value per share is calculated as follows:

Book Value per Share =
(Total Shareholders' Equity – Preferred Stock) / Outstanding Common Shares

Dividends

Dividends are declared by the board of directors and paid to stockholders. In order to pay cash dividends, the corporation must have enough cash and sufficient retained earnings. The declaration of a dividend lowers the company's retained earnings balance, and the theory is that dividends are a sharing of earnings with the stockholders.

The **dividend payout ratio** is the percentage of net income that is paid to stockholders and is calculated using this formula:

Dividends Paid During a Year / Net Income for that Same Year = Dividend Payout Ratio

The **earnings retention ratio** is the percentage of net income retained by the company and is calculated as follows:

Earnings Retention Ratio = 1 – Dividend Payout Percentage

Preferred Stock

Preferred stock gives its owners preferential treatment in a few ways. Although it usually carries no voting rights (stockholders can't vote for directors or other major corporate governance issues), preferred stock does have a superior priority over common stock in the payment of dividends and upon liquidation. Preferred stockholders will be paid out in assets before common stockholders and after debt holders in bankruptcy. Preferred stock may also have a **convertibility** feature, which means that the stock can be converted into common stock.

A hybrid between a bond and a stock, preferred stock has characteristics similar to each of those types of securities. Like a bond, preferred stockholders do not participate in earnings and dividend growth and you rarely see any growth of preferred stock value (unless it is convertible into common stock) as you would see with the price of the common stock issued by a profitable company. But preferred stock usually pays a fixed dividend—much like the way a bond pays a fixed amount of interest to the bondholders. The dividend is either specified as a percentage of the par value or as a fixed dollar amount per share. That idea of a constant cash flow helps make preferred stock a low-risk investment.

A preferred stock issue may also have cumulative, participating, and/or convertible features.
- **Cumulative:** dividends accrue if they are not paid on time and must be paid before common stockholders receive a dividend

- **Participating:** stockholders are given a right to participate in earnings or value over and above the stated dividend rate
- **Convertible:** shares can be converted for common stock or into some other stock or debt instrument

How to Value Preferred Stock

The value of a share of preferred stock is derived from the following formula:

Value of Preferred Share =
Annual Dividend / Required Dividend Yield (Required Rate of Return)

For example, if a preferred stock pays $10 per share and the investors required rate of return is 10 percent, then the stock would be valued at $100 ($10 / 0.10).

The **preferred stock valuation formula** is the same as that of a perpetual annuity (perpetuity). A **perpetual annuity** is a stream of equal payments that lasts "forever," or at least indefinitely. The formula for the value of a perpetual annuity is as follows:

Price of Preferred Stock (per Share) $- D / r$

Where:
- D is the periodic payment (the dividend)
- r is the required rate of return

For example, if the dividend on a preferred stock is $5 per share and the required rate of return is 6%, then the value of the share would be $83.33($5.00 / 0.06 = $83.33).

US Stock Indices

A **stock index** is a hypothetical portfolio of common stock holdings. The calculation of the index value comes from the prices of the underlying holdings and some type of weighting methodology such as market-capitalization proportions. **Market capitalization** refers to the total dollar market value of a company's outstanding shares. Also called **market cap**, market capitalization is calculated by multiplying a company's shares outstanding by the current market price of one share.

Common stock investors follow market indices in order to gauge the performance of their investments. The performance of a stock index is referred to as the performance of the market. For example, when an analyst states that the market was up 10%, it is probably the rate of return on an index such as the S&P 500.

The three major stock indices in the United States are as follows:

- **Dow Jones Industrial Average (also known as the Dow):** measures the daily stock price movements of 30 large, publicly owned US companies
- **Nasdaq Composite:** contains all of the companies (more than 3,000) that trade on the Nasdaq and are mostly technology and internet-related companies and to a lesser extent financial, consumer, biotech, and industrial companies as well
- **Standard & Poor's 500 Index (also called the S&P 500):** a composite of the 500 largest US publicly traded companies

CAPITAL BUDGETING

Capital budgeting is a process used by large companies for evaluating and ranking potential capital expenditures. Examples of capital expenditures include the following:

- Purchase of new equipment
- Rebuilding existing equipment
- Purchasing delivery vehicles
- Constructing additions to buildings

The steps in the capital budgeting process are as follows:

1. Identify possible projects.
2. Decide on appropriate projects to pursue.
3. Estimate initial cash outlays.
4. Estimate periodic cash outflows and periodic benefits.
5. Assess risk.
6. Evaluate and rank alternatives.
7. Implement acceptable projects.

Capital Asset

A **capital asset** is property that is expected to generate value and contribute to operations over a period of time greater than a year and beyond the current operating cycle. Capital assets form the productive capacity of a company—i.e., the permanent foundation of the business. Capital asset expenditures are different from operating expenditures. Operating expenditures, such as those for repairs and maintenance, only benefit the company during the current period, whereas a capital expenditure is made to acquire a long-term asset or significant improvements to currently owned long-term assets, such as investments that extend the life of the assets or add significant other benefits.

Usually financed with long-term sources of funds, such as long-term bank loans, bonds, preferred stock, and common stock, capital assets include buildings, equipment, tools, and vehicles. Capital assets are significant investments and will have a long-term impact on a company. As such, capital asset purchases should not be made until after related project cash flow forecasts are made and financial analysis tools have been used to help assure that only critical projects and projects with the best chance to help the company create wealth are chosen.

Project Cash Flow Forecasting and Analysis

When projecting cash flows related to capital asset projects, the initial cash outlay and the periodic cash flows (benefits) must be estimated. A **relevant cash flow** will change the company's overall future cash flow and occurs as a direct consequence of the decision to adopt the project.

A **sunk cost** is one that will occur or has occurred regardless of the decision to accept or reject a capital asset investment proposal. A sunk cost cash flow is an expenditure that is irrelevant to the capital asset investment decision. However, any opportunity cost related to the acceptance of a capital asset acquisition or project is relevant. If a decision results in losing out on or foregoing a future financial benefit, then that loss of benefit is called an opportunity cost.

Financial Analysis Tools

The following four capital budgeting techniques are utilized by financial managers:

1. Payback period
2. Net Present Value (NPV)
3. Internal Rate of Return (IRR)
4. Accounting Rate of Return (ARR)

The payback period tells you how long it will take to recover the initial investment. NPV determines whether a project earns more or less than a desired rate of return (also called the discount rate or cost of capital) and is good at finding out whether a project is going to help create wealth within the enterprise. IRR goes one step further than NPV to determine a specific rate of return for a project. Both NPV and IRR give you numbers that you can use to compare competing projects and make the best choice for your business. The accounting rate of return, the ARR, is calculated by dividing the average cash inflows by the cost.

Payback Period

The **payback period** is the number of years required to return the original investment. Companies that use the payback period method of analysis set a maximum length of time that projects must pay for themselves. If the cash flows are consistent each year, the payback period can be calculated as follows:

Payback Period = Initial Investment / Annual Expected Cash Flow

If the cash flows are not consistent each year, a running total of annual cash flows must be calculated to the point where those accumulated cash flows equal the initial investment. The limitations of the payback period are that it does not take into account the time value of money and that it disregards cash flows that occur after the payback period.

Net Present Value

The **net present value method** discounts the future cash flows related to a capital project and subtracts that number (the present value of the future benefits) from the initial investment. The discounting is done with a hurdle rate (usually the company's cost of capital). Here is the formula:

Net Present Value (NPV) =
Discounted Future Cash Flows – Initial Investment

If the NPV is positive, the project may be accepted as it is assumed to add to the value of the firm. If the NPV is negative, the project would probably be rejected (unless there are other compelling reasons to accept), as it would not cover the cost of capital and therefore would decrease the wealth of the firm.

Internal Rate of Return

The **internal rate of return (IRR)** expresses a project's return with a percentage. For example, a project with an IRR of 12% is expected to return 12% per year. The IRR is the discount rate that results in a net present value equal to zero. If the IRR is greater than the company's desired return, then the project may be accepted.

Accounting Rate of Return

The **Accounting Rate of Return (ARR)** is calculated by dividing the average annual cash inflows by the cost. The ARR does not take into account the time value of money.

Break Even and Sensitivity Analysis

At the **break-even point**, total revenue is exactly equal to total costs. Many people think of the break-even point as a type of hurdle, one that, once cleared, opens the door to profitability and corporate wealth building.

Business plans often include break-even analysis, as potential investors and creditors will factor the break-even point into their analysis as they contemplate the viability of the business and the plausibility of the assumptions upon which the business plan is based. For an entity that is already up and running and operating above the break-even point, the break-even point can represent a margin of safety as it allows you to answer the question, "How far can the output or revenue level fall before the entity reaches its break-even point?"

The break-even point model makes some basic assumptions. It assumes that you can clearly segregate costs into two categories—fixed and variable—and the behavior of these costs will remain unchanged over a relevant range of activity (a range of production and sales). It also assumes that the quantity of goods produced is equal to the quantity of goods sold.

A version of break-even analysis is **cost-volume-profit (CVP)** analysis—a tool that allows you to ask "what if" with regards to cost alternatives, varying sales and revenue volumes, and profit targets. Break-even quantity is calculated by this equation:

Break-Even Point (in Units) =
Total Fixed Costs / (Selling Price – Variable Costs per Unit)

The break-even formula can also be used to estimate the volume needed to achieve a target profit:

Volume (in Units) Needed to Achieve a Target Profit =
(Total Fixed Costs + Target Profit) / (Selling Price – Variable Costs per Unit)

COST OF CAPITAL

The **cost of capital** is the after-tax cost of the capital structure of an enterprise. It is not the cost of one component; rather, it is the cost of the blend of long-term financing—long-term loans, bonds, preferred stock, and equity—used by an organization.

In a business, the cost of capital is an important rate—a kind of hurdle—that should be surpassed on a consistent basis when investing in projects. The theory is that as long as the rates of return on investments made by the firm equal the cost of capital, market value will be maintained.

If the rate of return on capital investments surpasses the cost of capital hurdle, the market value of the firm will increase. The opposite is also true: if the rate of return on a capital asset is less than the cost of capital, the company's wealth will diminish as a result of that investment.

Cost of Debt

Debt capital with its interest payments is almost always a fixed cost source of funds. One important consideration when estimating the cost of debt is that interest expenses are tax deductible. The cost of long-term debt is the after-tax cost of raising long-term funds through borrowing—be it through bank loans or by floating bonds.

The after-tax cost of a bond is similar but a bit more complicated. The true cost of the bond is the yield to maturity. The after-tax cost of a bond is found with this formula:

$$\text{Yield to maturity} \times (1 - T)$$

Where:
- T is the firm's tax rate

Cost of Equity

The cost of equity is a two-part process of estimating the cost of preferred stock and then estimating the cost of common equity.

Preferred stock is a special type of ownership interest in a corporation. Preferred stockholders have the right to receive stated dividends before any earnings can be distributed to common stockholders. In some ways, preferred stock is a lot like bonds. Preferred stock usually has a fairly stable market value (share price) and the dividends are fixed—much like the coupon interest payments on bonds.

Preferred stock dividends can be stated as an amount, such as $5.00 per share, or as a percentage of a par value, such as 8 percent of $60, which would be $4.80 per share. Since par value never changes, even the preferred stock dividend that is a function (or percentage) of par is fixed.

Unless otherwise specified, preferred stock has an indefinite holding period so that when you estimate the cost of preferred stock you only consider the dividends. Therefore, if the dividend of the stock is $4.00 per share and the current price of the stock is $40, the cost of the preferred stock is 10 percent, found as follows:

$$D / P = \text{Cost of Preferred Stock}$$

Where:
- D is the preferred dividend
- P is the current market price per share of the stock

For the example given:

$$\$4.00 / \$40 = 10\%$$

The dividend is not tax deductible, so there is no adjustment to the cost of preferred stock, as is the case with the cost of debt.

Another way to estimate the cost of preferred stock is to calculate the cost as a percentage of the net proceeds from the sale of preferred stock. For example, if a company is looking to issue preferred stock at $90 per share with a $9.00 dividend, it would also need to estimate the **issuance cost per share** (also called **flotation costs**) to calculate the net proceeds:

$$\text{Net Proceeds per Share} = \text{Selling Price} - \text{Issuance Costs per Share}$$

For example, if you assume that the issuance costs are $3.00 per share, the cost of the preferred stock would be 10.3 percent, calculated as follows:

$$\text{Dividend per Share} / \text{Net Proceeds per Share}$$

The cost of **common stock** is the required return that investors in the market require. The theory is that investors have some required return that is used to discount the expected future cash flows of the stock to derive a value. The challenge is to estimate that expected return. One way is to use a derivative of the constant-growth valuation model.

The following **constant-growth model** formula can be used to estimate the cost of common stock:

$$\text{Cost} = \frac{D}{P + g}$$

Where:

- D is the dividend per share of the common stock
- P is the current price (market value) per share
- g is the estimated annual growth rate of the dividend

For example, if a common stock pays an $8.00 dividend per share, is selling for $100 per share, and has an annual dividend growth rate of 5 percent, the cost of the common stock would be estimated at 13 percent:

$$\$8 \,/\, \$100 + 0.05 = .08 + 0.05 = 13\%$$

The **capital asset pricing model (CAPM)** is another method that is used to calculate the cost of common stock. CAPM describes the relationship between risk and expected return and is used in estimating the value of risky securities, such as common stock. Here is the basic formula:

$$\text{Expected Rate of Return of Common Stock} = R_f + [b \times (k_m - R_f)]$$

Where:

- R_f is the risk-free rate of return
- b is the beta of the stock—i.e., a measure of risk
- k_m is the expected market return on common stock

For example, if the risk-free rate is 3 percent, the beta (risk measure) of the stock is 2, and the expected market return over the period is 10 percent, the stock is expected to return 17 percent, calculated as follows:

$$3\% + [2 \times (10\% - 3\%)] = 17\%$$

The beta for a stock is calculated using regression analysis and is published for most actively traded stocks by a number of investment research services, such as Value Line. The beta is an indication of price volatility relative to the market as a whole. The whole market is usually the S&P 500, which is assigned a beta of 1. The S&P 500 is a stock price index comprising the 500 largest companies in the United States.

Stocks that have a beta greater than 1 have greater price volatility than the overall market and are riskier. Stocks with a beta of 1 fluctuate in price at the same rate as the market. Stocks, with a beta of less than 1, have less price volatility than the market and are less risky.

The **cost of retained earnings** is essentially the same as the cost of common stock. Retained earnings are profits that were not paid out as dividends, and as such should earn at least a rate of return equal to the expected rate of return on the common stock. Otherwise, the common stockholders would be better off if the earnings were paid to them as opposed to being reinvested in the corporation.

Weighted Average Cost of Capital

The **weighted-average cost of capital** (**WACC**) is a single rate based on the combined components of a firm's capital. Management may set certain targets (weights) for each component of capital and use those weights when calculating the WACC. The cost for each component of capital in the weighted average cost of capital calculation is usually the marginal cost of capital, the cost of the last dollar of new capital that the firm raises.

RISK AND RETURN

There is a **risk/return trade-off** that all investors must consider when committing dollars to an investment. Investors must seek to balance the amount of risk they are willing to assume with the desire to maximize returns. Investors seeking higher returns usually assume higher risks. Risk adverse investors usually settle for lower returns in safer investment alternatives. Investments in US treasury securities carry low risk but there is no potential for high returns, whereas an investment in a speculative common stock issue may provide high investment yields, but it also carries high risk.

Expected Return on an Asset and a Portfolio

The **expected return** of an asset (investment) is the average of possible outcomes according to their probabilities. For example, if there are two possibilities, a 50% return with an 80% probability and a 40% loss with a 20% probability, then the expected return is 34% (50% × 0.8 + 30% × 0.2). The expected return of a portfolio is based on the expected return and weight of each asset in a portfolio. Each asset's weight is multiplied by its expected return, and then those results are summed to derive the expected return of the portfolio.

Measures of Risk

Two measures of investment risk are the **standard deviation** of returns and an investment's **beta**. The standard deviation (variance) of the distribution of the investment returns is a statistic that measures the dispersion of the data set relative to its mean (average rate of return). It measures the "tightness" of the distribution of an investment's historical returns around a mean (average return of the investment.) The standard deviation of an investment's return is an indication of investment value volatility.

Despite the fact that the standard deviation of an investment's returns is an indication of an investment's risk, the risk of a portfolio of stocks is usually not the average of the standard deviation of the particular stocks in the portfolio. The effect of diversification results in a portfolio that has less risk than would be measured by the average of the standard deviations of the stocks in that portfolio.

Another risk measure is the **coefficient of variation**, which is calculated by dividing the standard deviation by the expected value. When comparing the coefficient of variation of two investments, the larger coefficient means more risk.

Beta is another statistic that measures an investment's sensitivity to movements of value in the overall market. A stock with a beta of 1 moves in a similar manner to the market, and if the market is up 10%, a stock with a beta of 1 will probably also be up about 10% (or down 10%, if the market is down 10%). A beta of less than 1 means the investment has moved in a less volatile manner than the market's movements, and a beta that is greater than 1 means the investment has shown more volatility than the overall market.

Determinants of Interest Rates

A **nominal interest rate** is the rate on a savings account, certificate of deposit, investment (such as the current yield on a bond), or loan before taking inflation into account. Many factors influence nominal interest rates, including the demand for money, conditions in both the money and capital markets, inflation expectations, and other development in the economy.

Real interest rates are inflation adjusted rates. For example, if a one-year certificate of deposit is paying a nominal rate of 8% and inflation is running at 5%, then the real interest rate is 3% (8% − 5%).

Capital Asset Pricing Model (CAPM) and Security Market Line (SML)

The CAPM quantifies the required return on an equity security by relating the security's level of risk to the average return of the market. The formula is as follows:

$$\text{Required Rate of Return} = R_f + b\,(R_m - R_f)$$

Where:
- R_f is the risk-free rate of return
- b is the beta of the investment
- R_m is the market return

The last part of the formula, $b\,(R_m - R_f)$, incorporates a risk premium into the required return.

The **security market line** is a chart produced from the CAPM and allows you to see a graphical representation of the risk-free return and the market risk premium of an expected rate of return.

Diversification

All investments carry some risk. Two basic risks are market risk and company-specific risk. **Market risk**, also called **systematic risk**, is risk that is attributable to market factors that are beyond the control of a company and tend to affect all firms. Factors such as wars, economic downturns (e.g., recessions and depressions), inflation, and political events are all part of market risk. Market risk is difficult to reduce via diversification, and it is sometimes referred to as **nondiversifiable risk**. For example, during bear markets, most well diversified stock funds show losses.

Company-specific risk, also called **unsystematic risk**, is attributable to factors related to a certain company. For example, specific risk would be present if there is a chance that a particular company's work force will go on strike and profits will be negatively impacted. Company-specific risk is referred to as **diversifiable risk**.

Portfolio Risk

When combining investments into a portfolio, the risk of any single investment cannot be reviewed independently of the other assets in the portfolio. Investments in a portfolio must be viewed in light of their impact on the risk and return of the portfolio.

Correlation is a statistical measure of the relationship between the returns of assets. To reduce overall risk, investment managers combine or add investments to a portfolio that are negatively correlated. The degree of correlation is measured by the **correlation coefficient**. For example, if two investment values move in the same direction, they are considered positively correlated. If their values move in opposite directions, they are negatively correlated. In other words:

- A **+1 correlation coefficient** equals a perfect correlation between two investments, meaning the investments are moving in the same direction.
- A **−1 correlation coefficient** equals a perfect negative correlation, meaning the investments are moving in opposite directions.

Some investments are **uncorrelated**, meaning there is no correlation—positive or negative—between their returns. Combining uncorrelated investments can also reduce the risk of a portfolio. As a general rule, the lower the correlation between investment returns within a portfolio, the greater the chance of diversification of risk.

INTERNATIONAL FINANCIAL MANAGEMENT

International financial management presents challenges that are different from domestic finance. The most significant challenge is risk as a result of foreign currency exposure. **Exchange rate risk**, also known as **currency risk**, arises from the change in the price of one currency in relation to another currency. For example, if a company owns assets in another country or owns assets that are denominated in a foreign country's currency, the values of those assets can fall because of changes in exchange rates.

Factors that affect exchange rates include the following:

- Relative inflation rates (between two countries)
- Government intervention that impacts exchange rates
- Relative interest rates (between two countries)

An **exchange rate** is the value of one country's currency for the purpose of conversion to another country's currency. The spot rate is the number of units of a foreign currency that can be received today in exchange for a single unit of a domestic currency. For example, if a US businessperson is willing to pay one US dollar for 1.3 British pounds, then the spot rate for the pound is 1.3 (relative to the US dollar).

Foreign currency exchange rates also can affect capital asset budgeting decisions. For example, when a US-based company is evaluating an investment in a capital project located in a foreign country where euros are the currency and the cash flows would be in euros, in calculating the net present value of the project the current spot rate would be used to convert the initial investment into dollars, and estimates of a future exchange rate would be needed to convert the future euro cash flows into dollars.

There is no single location for foreign exchange as the market is a network of financial institutions and participants located all over the globe. Exchange rate risk is not the only risk of international operations. **Political risk** is the type of risk that evaluates how political decisions, events, or conditions will affect a company's profitability.

International financial management involves the use of various strategies and tools to manage risk. **Hedging** involves mitigating the risks of foreign exchange. When hedging a foreign exchange risk, a number of tools are available to financial managers to reduce the risk of receivables and payables. Those tools include **currency options** and **forward contracts**. There are two types of options: call and put. A **call option** gives the holder the right to buy a specified amount of currency in a future month at a set price. A call option is a hedge for accounts payable risks. A **put option** gives the holder the right to seek a specified amount of currency in a future month at a specified price and is a hedge against receivable risks of foreign exchange.

A **forward currency contract** (also called a **futures contract**) is an agreement to exchange one currency for another at a specified date in the future at a price (exchange rate) that is fixed on the purchase date of this foreign exchange derivative. A **forward rate** is the number of units of a foreign currency that can be exchanged for a single unit of the domestic currency at some definite date in the future.

A **financial derivative,** like a foreign exchange futures contract, is an agreement between two or more parties whose value is based on an agreed-upon underlying financial asset or an index. Common underlying instruments include bonds, commodities, currencies, interest rates, market indexes, and stocks.

SUMMING IT UP

- **Financial statements** are prepared at the end of an accounting cycle to communicate and evaluate results of operations, financial position, and cash flow activity of a business.
- Summarizing results from past periods, the **income statement** and the **statement of cash flows** reveal revenues, expenses, and the sources and uses of cash, respectively, covering a specified period.
- The **balance sheet** reveals details about liquidity, solvency, financial flexibility, risk, and the sources of funds for the assets of a company.
- **Time value of money** calculations are used when computing compounding of interest on a savings account, calculating the annual rate of return on an equity mutual fund, calculating a loan payment, and evaluating the projected cash flows from a capital project.
- Loan amortizations, lease payments, and bond interest rates are all related to the principles of the time value of money.
- An **interest rate** is the charge by a lender to a borrower for the use of money and is based on a 12-month period.
- **Budgets** are prepared with a comparison to actual results and the calculation of variances—i.e., the difference between the budgeted amount and the actual amount.
- The **operating budget** is a collection of budgets, including those for revenues (sales), cash needs, production, selling and administrative expenses, and purchases.
- A **bond** is a debt security that involves lending money to a government, municipality, federal agency, or corporation—known as the **bond issuer**—in return for payment of a specified rate of interest to the investor during the life of the bond and repayment of the face value of the bond (the principal) when it "matures" (comes due).
- **Common and preferred stock** are forms of equity in a corporation. A preferred stock is a hybrid form of ownership, as the preferred stock is more like a bond investment, while a common stock is a truer form of ownership.
- **Capital budgeting** is a process used by large companies for evaluating and ranking potential capital expenditures.
- The **cost of capital** is the cost of the blend of long-term financing—long-term loans, bonds, preferred stock, and equity—used by an organization.
- Investors must seek to balance the amount of **risk** they are willing to assume with the desire to maximize returns.
- **International financial management** presents challenges, such as **currency risk**, which arises from the change in the price of one currency in relation to another currency, and involves various strategies and tools to manage risk, such as hedging, forward currency contracts, and financial derivatives.

Chapter 4

Principles of Finance Post-Test

POST-TEST ANSWER SHEET

1. Ⓐ Ⓑ Ⓒ Ⓓ   16. Ⓐ Ⓑ Ⓒ Ⓓ   31. Ⓐ Ⓑ Ⓒ Ⓓ

2. Ⓐ Ⓑ Ⓒ Ⓓ   17. Ⓐ Ⓑ Ⓒ Ⓓ   32. Ⓐ Ⓑ Ⓒ Ⓓ

3. Ⓐ Ⓑ Ⓒ Ⓓ   18. Ⓐ Ⓑ Ⓒ Ⓓ   33. Ⓐ Ⓑ Ⓒ Ⓓ

4. Ⓐ Ⓑ Ⓒ Ⓓ   19. Ⓐ Ⓑ Ⓒ Ⓓ   34. Ⓐ Ⓑ Ⓒ Ⓓ

5. Ⓐ Ⓑ Ⓒ Ⓓ   20. Ⓐ Ⓑ Ⓒ Ⓓ   35. Ⓐ Ⓑ Ⓒ Ⓓ

6. Ⓐ Ⓑ Ⓒ Ⓓ   21. Ⓐ Ⓑ Ⓒ Ⓓ   36. Ⓐ Ⓑ Ⓒ Ⓓ

7. Ⓐ Ⓑ Ⓒ Ⓓ   22. Ⓐ Ⓑ Ⓒ Ⓓ   37. Ⓐ Ⓑ Ⓒ Ⓓ

8. Ⓐ Ⓑ Ⓒ Ⓓ   23. Ⓐ Ⓑ Ⓒ Ⓓ   38. Ⓐ Ⓑ Ⓒ Ⓓ

9. Ⓐ Ⓑ Ⓒ Ⓓ   24. Ⓐ Ⓑ Ⓒ Ⓓ   39. Ⓐ Ⓑ Ⓒ Ⓓ

10. Ⓐ Ⓑ Ⓒ Ⓓ   25. Ⓐ Ⓑ Ⓒ Ⓓ   40. Ⓐ Ⓑ Ⓒ Ⓓ

11. Ⓐ Ⓑ Ⓒ Ⓓ   26. Ⓐ Ⓑ Ⓒ Ⓓ   41. Ⓐ Ⓑ Ⓒ Ⓓ

12. Ⓐ Ⓑ Ⓒ Ⓓ   27. Ⓐ Ⓑ Ⓒ Ⓓ   42. Ⓐ Ⓑ Ⓒ Ⓓ

13. Ⓐ Ⓑ Ⓒ Ⓓ   28. Ⓐ Ⓑ Ⓒ Ⓓ   43. Ⓐ Ⓑ Ⓒ Ⓓ

14. Ⓐ Ⓑ Ⓒ Ⓓ   29. Ⓐ Ⓑ Ⓒ Ⓓ   44. Ⓐ Ⓑ Ⓒ Ⓓ

15. Ⓐ Ⓑ Ⓒ Ⓓ   30. Ⓐ Ⓑ Ⓒ Ⓓ   45. Ⓐ Ⓑ Ⓒ Ⓓ

46. Ⓐ Ⓑ Ⓒ Ⓓ   51. Ⓐ Ⓑ Ⓒ Ⓓ   56. Ⓐ Ⓑ Ⓒ Ⓓ

47. Ⓐ Ⓑ Ⓒ Ⓓ   52. Ⓐ Ⓑ Ⓒ Ⓓ   57. Ⓐ Ⓑ Ⓒ Ⓓ

48. Ⓐ Ⓑ Ⓒ Ⓓ   53. Ⓐ Ⓑ Ⓒ Ⓓ   58. Ⓐ Ⓑ Ⓒ Ⓓ

49. Ⓐ Ⓑ Ⓒ Ⓓ   54. Ⓐ Ⓑ Ⓒ Ⓓ   59. Ⓐ Ⓑ Ⓒ Ⓓ

50. Ⓐ Ⓑ Ⓒ Ⓓ   55. Ⓐ Ⓑ Ⓒ Ⓓ   60. Ⓐ Ⓑ Ⓒ Ⓓ

PRINCIPLES OF FINANCE POST-TEST
72 minutes—60 questions

Directions: Carefully read each of the following 60 questions. Choose the best answer to each question and fill in the corresponding circle on the answer sheet. The Answer Key and Explanations can be found following this post-test.

---

1. Which of the following is NOT a profitability ratio?

   A. Dividend yield
   B. Return on assets
   C. Gross profit percentage
   D. Net profit margin

2. The _____ budget is prepared after the operating budgets and the capital expenditures budget are prepared.

   A. sales
   B. purchases
   C. cash
   D. general and administrative

3. Which of the following has the most impact on short-term interest rates?

   A. Securities and Exchange Commission
   B. Small Business Administration
   C. Mortgage bankers
   D. Federal Reserve

4. A company currently has fixed costs of $1,000,000 and variable costs per unit of $10. Management wants to implement new strategic plans and, as a result, estimates that fixed costs will increase by a very significant amount of $530,000. The plan also calls for cost cutting to save $1 of variable costs per unit. If the company sells the project for $60 and implements the plans, what would be the new break-even point?

   A. 20,000
   B. 30,000
   C. 19,600
   D. 25,500

5. The use of futures contracts would most likely be used to

A. assure a profit.
B. hedge against losses.
C. maximize cash flow.
D. factor receivables.

6. What is the value of one share of common stock with an expected year-end dividend of $1.50 per share and an expected year-end selling price per share of $40, assuming that the holding period is just one year and the investor's expected rate of return is 15%?

A. $36.11
B. $38.50
C. $40.00
D. $41.50

7. A _____ ratio, such as the _____ ratio, measures a company's ability to meet long-term obligations.

A. liquidity; current
B. solvency; cash
C. solvency; times interest earned
D. profitability; return on equity

8. The CAPM quantifies the _____ on a(n) _____ security by relating the security's level of risk to the expected return of the market.

A. required return; equity
B. yield to maturity; bond
C. beta; equity
D. current income; bond

9. Bondholders provide capital funds with the expectation that the corporation will deploy those funds so that the bondholder will

A. receive a dividend based on the par value of the bond.
B. receive capital gains on the bond.
C. realize the yield to maturity on the bond.
D. realize an expected return greater than that earned by common stockholders.

10. When there is a net _____ in accounts receivable for the period, cash collected from customers is more than _____ and would be shown as an increase in cash from operating activities on the cash flow statement.

A. increase; revenues
B. increase; expenses
C. decrease; revenues
D. decrease; expenses

11. Which of the following is NOT an example of an inventory ordering cost?

A. Clerical cost of preparing a purchase order
B. Cost of the receiving function
C. Insurance costs of storing inventory
D. The cost of comparing the receipt of inventory against the purchase order

12. XYZ Corporation, with a 12% cost of capital, is considering a capital asset project with an expected life of 4 years. The project requires an initial cash outlay of $500,000 with the following expected future cash flows:

Year 1 $10,000

Year 2 $15,000

Year 3 $20,000

Year 4 $25,000

The following time value of money tables have been provided. (Use only the one relevant to this question.)

Present Value of $1	
Years	12%
1	0.893
2	0.797
3	0.712
4	0.636

Future Value of $1	
Years	12%
1	1.120
2	1.254
3	1.405
4	1.574

What is the NPV of the project, and should it be accepted or rejected based on these facts?

A. $51,010; Accept
B. $20,000; Reject
C. $1,010; Accept
D. $18,777; Reject

13. Which of the following best defines the average collection period?

    A. The average length of time (days) from the purchase order date till the goods are received

    B. The average length of time (days) from a sale on credit until the payment is received

    C. The average length of time (days) it takes to make a payment on an accounts payable

    D. The average length of time (days) from the time a bill collector contacts a firm for collection of a bill till the date the firm pays the bill

14. Capital budgeting analysis techniques such as NPV and IRR use which of the following to evaluate the acceptability of the project?

I. Cash inflows as a result of the project

II. Net income as a result of the project

III. Noncash expenses as a result of the project

IV. Cash outflows as a result of the project

    A. I and II
    B. II only
    C. I and IV
    D. III and IV

15. A particular bond that sells for $900 and a face value of $1,000 pays $45 semi-annually to its investors over a period of 10 years. What is the annual coupon rate of the bond?

    A. 4.5%
    B. 9%
    C. 10%
    D. 10.67%

16. Consider the information below regarding two investments:

Investment	Expected Value	Standard Deviation
A	$230,000	$107,700
B	$250,000	$206,000

Which of the following statements is true?

A. Investment A is less risky than Investment B because it has a lower coefficient of variation.

B. Investment B is less risky than Investment A because it has a lower coefficient of variance.

C. Investment B is riskier than Investment A because its expected value is greater.

D. Investment A is less risky than Investment B because its expected value is less.

Use the following tables to answer questions 17 and 18.

Present Value of $1		Present Value of a $1 Annuity	
Years	Interest rate = 10%	Years	Interest rate = 10%
1	0.9091	1	0.9091
2	0.8264	2	1.7355
3	0.7513	3	2.4869
4	0.6830	4	3.1699
5	0.6209	5	3.7908

17. A corporation anticipates that it will collect $100,000 on a note receivable in 5 years. Assuming a 10% annual interest rate, what is the discounted value (today value) of the note receivable? Please use the appropriate time value of money factor from the partial tables shown.

A. $62,090
B. $90,091
C. $173,550
D. $379,080

18. An investment is expected to produce annual cash flows of $20,000 for four years. What is its present value if an annual return of 10% is required?

A. $80,000
B. $75,816
C. $63,398
D. $13,660

19. Which of the following are reasons why providers of equity capital have a higher expected return, and therefore a higher cost of capital to the firm, than that of debt?

I. The corporation is not legally obligated to pay equity investors any rate of return.

II. In the case of liquidation, equity investors are situated behind debt holders in the order of liquidation.

III. The risk of investing in equities is lower than the risk of investing in bonds

IV. The interest rate risk of equities is higher than that of bonds.

A. I only
B. I and II
C. I, II, and III
D. I, II, III, IV

20. A partial table of present value interest factors is shown for a single amount. If the present value of $100,000 received in 5 years is equal to about $71,000, what is the estimated annual interest rate used to discount the $100,000?

Present Value of $1				
Years	5%	6%	7%	8%
5	0.7835	0.7473	0.7130	0.6806

A. 5%
B. 6%
C. 7%
D. 8%

21. _____ are increases in assets from the major or central ongoing operations of a business and are reported on the _____.

A. Accounts receivables; balance sheet
B. Cash inflows; income statement
C. Net Income; retained earnings statement
D. Revenues; income statement

22. Earnings per share is typically reported on the face of which of the following financial statements?

A. Income statement
B. Balance sheet
C. Statement of stockholders' equity
D. Cash flow statement

23. If a company wants to accumulate $1,000,000 in a sinking fund to pay off a debt by investing an amount today, which time value of money concept would be useful in determining the amount?

A. Present value of a $1 annuity
B. Present value of a $1
C. Future value of a $1
D. Future value of a $1 annuity

24. Which of the following accurately describes the cash cycle (in days)?

    A. The period between when a company purchases inventory and pays its suppliers
    B. The number of days that inventory is in stock before it is sold
    C. The period of time between when a company pays its suppliers and collects from its customers
    D. The number of days it takes to collect on accounts receivable balances owed by customers

25. When calculating a bond's value based on the basic bond valuation model (present value of future cash flows), which of the following factors must be known?

    I. Amounts of cash flow (interest and principal) to be received by the bondholder

    II. Bondholder's other investments including the risk levels of those investments (i.e., betas on the stocks)

    III. Maturity date of the bond

    IV. Investor's required annual return

    A. I, III, and IV only
    B. I only
    C. I and II only
    D. I, II, III, and IV

26. In a cash budget, the beginning cash balance is added to the projected cash inflows and then the cash outflows are subtracted. If that amount is less than the company's required minimum balance of cash, what will the financing section of the cash budget show?

    A. Surplus
    B. Net income
    C. Borrowings needed
    D. Net loss

27. If the foreign earnings are a high percentage of net income of a particular company, it could be said that the company is subject to a high level of

    A. currency risk.
    B. inflation risk.
    C. interest rate risk.
    D. liquidity risk.

28. A company is considering introducing a new product line with an initial investment of $250,000. Expected relevant net cash inflows are $80,000 for the next 5 years. Management wants its money back in 4 years. Based on these facts, what is the payback period and is the project acceptable (accept) or will it be rejected (reject)?

    A. 1 year; accept
    B. 2.1 years; reject
    C. 3.125 years; accept
    D. 4 years; reject

29. Which of the following ratios is NOT used in the DuPont model?

    A. Current assets / current liabilities
    B. Net profit margin
    C. Total asset turnover
    D. Total assets / total stockholders' equity

30. Diversification is a _____ technique that involves choosing a variety of investments for inclusion into a portfolio so that positive performances of some investments compensate for negative or low performance of the other investments in the portfolio.

    A. leveraging
    B. speculative
    C. hedging
    D. tax advantaged

31. Mary pays 15% percent of her income in income taxes (total taxes owed / taxable income), yet on each additional dollar she earns she must pay an additional 20 cents in taxes. Which of the following statements is true?

A. Her marginal tax rate and her average tax rate are equal to 20%.
B. Her average tax rate is equal to 15%, and her marginal tax rate is equal to 20%.
C. Her marginal tax rate is equal to 15%, and her average tax rate is equal to 20%.
D. Her marginal tax rate and her average tax rate are equal to 15%.

32. Which of the following ratios is also called the acid test?

A. Current ratio
B. Cash ratio
C. Cash coverage ratio
D. Quick ratio

33. Which of the following formulas would be used to calculate the current cost of capital raised for retained earnings?

A. Next dividend / net issue proceeds
B. Annual interest / net issue proceeds
C. Yield to maturity × (1 – tax rate)
D. (Next dividend / net proceeds) + Dividend growth rate

34. A company's capital structure and estimated costs are shown below.

Capital	Amounts	Cost
Debt	$500,000	10% (1)
Preferred Stock	$600,000	12% (2)
Common Stock	$900,000	15% (3)

(1) Yield to maturity
(2) Current yield
(3) Based on the constant dividend growth model

What is the cost of capital if the company's marginal tax rate is 21%?
A. 7.9%
B. 11.63%
C. 12.325%
D. 15%

35. Ralph will deposit $10,000 per year into an investment account that earns 8% per year for 10 years. What will be the account value after 10 years?

Future Value of $1	
Years	8%
10	2.159%

Future Value of Annuity	
Years	8%
10	14.487%

A. $166,450
B. $144,870
C. $108,000
D. $21,590

36. Which of the following is the commonly used basis for the calculation of the capital cost of a bond?

A. Coupon rate adjusted for income taxes
B. Current yield
C. Yield to maturity adjusted for income taxes
D. Yield to maturity

37. An annuity arrangement will pay its owner $10,000 a year at the end of each year for 5 years. Assuming an annual interest rate of 8%, what is the present value of that arrangement? Use one of the following factors to determine the answer.

Ordinary annuity future value factor	5.867
Annuity due future value factor	6.336
Ordinary annuity present value factor	3.993
Annuity due present value factor	4.312

A. $63,360
B. $58,670
C. $43,120
D. $39,930

38. Last year, a corporation purchased $1,000,000 of its own stock and has not reissued the stock. When issuing its most recent set of financial statements, what statement would show that stock transaction, and within which section of that financial statement will it be shown?

A. Balance sheet, equity section
B. Balance sheet, current assets
C. Income statement, expenses
D. Retained earnings, dividends declared

39. In an initial public offering, Jim buys 100 shares of $6 par value XYZ common stock for $5,000. The company's equity is listed on the balance sheet at a total of $5,000,000, while its preferred stock is listed for $500,000. There are 100,000 shares of XYZ stock outstanding. What is the book value per share of the XYZ common stock?

A. $50
B. $45
C. $44
D. $6

40. Consider the following portfolio:

Investments	Amount	Expected return of each asset
A	$500,000	15%
B	$200,000	6%
C	$300,000	9%

What is the expected return?
A. 10%
B. 11.4%
C. 15%
D. 30%

41. A customer purchases $10,000 of product from Company A with credit terms of 2/10, net 30. At the end of the month, this is the only amount owed to Company A. On which month-end financial statement will this appear?

A. Statement of cash flows
B. Balance sheet
C. Retained earnings statement
D. Statement of stockholders' equity

42. Which of the following would be an appropriate strategy for managing the cash conversion cycle?

A. Pay accounts payable as slowly as possible without damaging the firm's credit rating and without foregoing significant purchase discounts.
B. Pay accounts payable as soon as the invoice is received so as to maintain a stellar payment history.
C. Turn over inventory slowly so as to not incur stockouts and lost sales.
D. Allow customers more generous credit terms than competitors so as to increase sales.

43. If Cynthia deposits $5,000 into an investment account that earns 8% per year, what will be the account's value at the end of 10 years? The following future value factors are derived from time value of money tables. Be sure to choose the appropriate factor.

Future Value of $1	
Years	8%
10	2.159%

Future Value of Annuity	
Years	8%
10	14.487%

A. $72,435
B. $50,000
C. $10,795
D. $5,400

44. A company borrows $100,000 at an interest rate of 1.5 above the prime rate, which is 9%. Interest will be paid at the end of 12 months. Every 90 days (each quarter), the interest that has accrued will be added to the principal loan balance. What is the effective annual rate of interest in this loan?

A. 2.625%
B. 9%
C. 10.5%
D. 10.92%

45. What is the last expense shown on an income statement?

A. Cost of goods sold
B. Depreciation
C. Interest
D. Income tax

46. A partial table of present value interest factors for an ordinary annuity is shown. If the present value of a 5-year, $10,000 annuity ($10,000 payment each year for 5 years) is about $42,000, what is the annual interest rate?

Present Value of $1 Annuity				
Years	5%	6%	7%	8%
5	4.329	4.21	4.100	3.993

A. 5%
B. 6%
C. 7%
D. 8%

47. An investment requires an initial investment of $50,000 and has the following future net cash inflows:

Year 1 $10,000

Year 2 $15,000

Year 3 $20,000

Year 4 $25,000

Using the given table, what is the estimate of the Internal Rate of Return (IRR) of this investment?

Years	10%	11%	12%	13%
1	0.909	0.901	0.893	0.885
2	0.826	0.812	0.797	0.783
3	0.751	0.731	0.712	0.693
4	0.683	0.659	0.636	0.613

A. Between 10% and 11%
B. Between 11% and 12%
C. Between 12% and 13%
D. More than 13%

48. If the term structure of interest rates shows the following rates and maturities, which of the following choices would describe the line chart/graphic depiction (of the term structure of interest rates)?

Promissory Notes
Years to maturity 2 years, interest rate 6%
Years to maturity 10 years, interest rate 7%
Years to maturity, 15 years 8.5%

A. Upward sloping
B. Flat
C. Downward sloping
D. Humped

49. Review the following capital structure.

Component	Amount
10% Bonds Payable	$5,000,000
11% Preferred stock	$4,800,000
Common Stock	$12,000,000
Retained Earnings	$6,000,000
Total	$27,800,000

What is the proportion of equity?

A. 43%

B. 60%

C. 65%

D. 82%

50. An example of a market prospect ratio is

A. times interest earned.

B. current ratio.

C. net profit margin.

D. price/earnings (P/E) ratio.

51. The _____ rate is the exchange rate for later delivery of currency, whereas the _____ rate is for immediate delivery of currencies exchanged.

A. spot; forward

B. spot; bid

C. bid; ask

D. forward; spot

52. Which of the following formulas would be used to calculate the cost of new capital raised by the issuance of preferred stock?

A. Next dividend paid on a share of preferred stock / net issue proceeds per share

B. Annual interest paid on the preferred stock / net issue proceeds per share

C. Yield to maturity of the corporation's bonds × (1 − tax rate)

D. (Next dividend paid on a share of preferred stock /net proceeds per share) + dividend growth rate

53. The following are some facts about a three-year bond.

- Face Value = $1,000
- Required return (yield to maturity) for the bondholder = 9%
- Annual coupon rate = 6%

Time Value of Money Factors		
Present Value of $1		
Years	6%	9%
1	0.943	0.917
2	0.890	0.842
3	0.840	0.772
Present Value of Annuity		
Years	6%	9%
1	0.943	0.917
2	1.833	1.759
3	2.673	2.531

Using the time value of money factors that are given, what is the value of the bond? Assume the bond pays interest once a year and that the interest payments will start one (1) year from now.

A. $1,000.00

B. $923.86

C. $772.18

D. $666.67

54. The treasurer of a corporation deposits $50,000 each year for 10 years into an investment account that grows to $724,350 by the end of year 10. Using the partial time value of money table (for the future value of a $1.00 annuity) shown, estimate the annual rate of return earned on the investment.

Years	5%	6%	7%	8%
10	12.578	13.181	13.816	14.487

A. 5%
B. 6%
C. 7%
D. 8%

55. What is the value of one share of common stock that had a dividend of $3.00 paid at the end of the first year, an expected annual dividend growth rate of 10%, and an investor's expected rate of return of 12%?

A. $25.00
B. $27.50
C. $150.00
D. $165.00

56. Good Products Inc. borrowed $100,000 for one year and paid the total amount of $9,000 interest up front. The inflation rate at the time was 3%. What is the effective annual interest rate of the loan?

A. 9.89%
B. 9%
C. 6.89%
D. 6%

57. A company has fixed costs of $500,000 and estimates that its variable costs per unit are $10. If the company sells the product for $60, what is the break-even point in units and in revenue?

A. 10,000 units; $500,000
B. 10,000 units; $600,000
C. 8,333 units; $500,000
D. 8,333 units; $583,333

58. US corporations with international operations may opt to finance operations with foreign debt to

A. pay debts back in US dollars.
B. increase earnings per share.
C. avoid local currencies.
D. lessen currency exchange risk.

59. A corporation paid a $1.00 per share dividend on common stock during the past year and is expected to pay the same amount this year. The most recent earnings per share for the stock are $2.50. Its P/E ratio is 18, while the industry average P/E is 20. What is the per share price of the stock?

A. $18
B. $20
C. $45
D. $50

60. Using the partial table of future value interest factors of $1 shown, determine the approximate annual rate of return on an investment that involves an initial deposit of $20,000 and is worth $28,100 after 5 years.

Years	5%	6%	7%	8%
5	1.276	1.338	1.403	1.469

A. 5%
B. 6%
C. 7%
D. 8%

ANSWER KEY AND EXPLANATIONS

1. A	13. B	25. A	37. D	49. D
2. C	14. C	26. C	38. A	50. D
3. D	15. B	27. A	39. B	51. D
4. B	16. A	28. C	40. B	52. A
5. B	17. A	29. A	41. B	53. B
6. A	18. C	30. C	42. A	54. D
7. C	19. B	31. B	43. C	55. D
8. A	20. C	32. D	44. D	56. A
9. C	21. D	33. D	45. D	57. B
10. C	22. A	34. C	46. B	58. D
11. C	23. B	35. B	47. C	59. C
12. C	24. C	36. C	48. A	60. C

1. **The correct answer is A.** The dividend yield is a market ratio; it is helpful to investors because it reflects a return on investment, absent any capital gain or loss that might be experienced on the investment. Return on assets (choice B), gross profit margin (choice C), and net profit margin (choice D) are profitability ratios.

2. **The correct answer is C.** The cash budget is prepared after all the operating and capital asset acquisition budgets are prepared so that all projected cash needs can be considered. Choices A, B, and D are all a part of the operating budget and are prepared before the cash budget.

3. **The correct answer is D.** The Federal Reserve influences the federal funds rate, the interest rate that banks can charge other banks when they lend excess reserves. The federal funds rate has an impact on short-term interest rates such as the prime rate (the short-term interest rate that banks charge their best customers). Many short-term interest rates are impacted, linked to, or a function of the prime rate. The SEC (choice A) regulates the stock and bond markets and has nothing to do with setting interest rate policy. The main mission of the SBA (choice B) is to support the development of small businesses; it does not set or influence long-term or short-term interest rates. Choice C is incorrect because any influence that mortgage bankers might have on interest rates would be minimal and would be related to long-term mortgage rates.

4. The correct answer is B. The new break-even point is calculated as follows:

$$\$1,530,000 / (\$60 - \$9) = 30,000$$

Choice A is incorrect because the current break-even point is 20,000 units. Choices C and D don't accurately apply the "What if" analysis (sensitivity) by using correct inputs into the break-even formula. Choice C doesn't consider the increase in fixed costs, and choice D doesn't consider the lower contribution margin (selling price – variable costs).

5. The correct answer is B. A hedge is an investment to reduce the risk of adverse price movements in an asset. Hedging involves taking an offsetting position in a related security, which can be achieved in various ways, including options and futures contracts. Choice A is incorrect because the use of options and futures contracts are not a guarantee of a profit, nor are they a way to maximize cash flow from an investment, as choice C implies. Choice D is incorrect because factoring receivables is a technique a company may use to derive cash from its outstanding account receivables.

6. The correct answer is A. The formula for a valuation of a share of common stock with a 1-year holding period is Price = Dividend / $(1 + r)$ + Price at the end of the year / $(1 + r)$, where r is the expected rate of return. Therefore, $\$1.50 / (1 + 0.15) + \$40 / (1 + 0.15) = \$36.11$. Choice B is incorrect because $38.50 is the selling price less the dividend; however, the dividend and the selling price are both positive cash flows that need to be discounted using the required rate of return. Choice C is incorrect because $40 is the future value of the stock and not the present value of the future cash flows (dividend and selling price). Choice D is incorrect because $41.50 is the total of the future cash flows, whereas the value of the stock is the present value of the future cash flows.

7. **The correct answer is C.** Solvency is a company's ability to make its interest and principal payments on long-term debt. The times interest earned ratio is an example of a solvency ratio. Choice A is incorrect as liquidity refers to a company's ability to meet its short-term obligations. Choice B is incorrect because the cash ratio is a liquidity ratio. Choice D is incorrect because profitability ratios measure focus in net income and other measures of profit as those measures relate to other amounts reported on the financial statements.

8. **The correct answer is A.** The Capital Asset Pricing Model (CAPM) quantifies the required return on an equity security by relating the security's level of risk to the expected return of the market (portfolio). Choices B and D are incorrect because the CAPM is for equity (i.e., common stock) investments, not bonds. Beta (choice C) is a risk measure used in the CAPM model to calculate the required return.

9. **The correct answer is C.** The yield to maturity at the time the bond is purchased is the annual rate of return that a bondholder expects to realize on the investment. It takes into account the periodic interest and any premium or discount as a result of the bond's market value. Choice A is incorrect because only stockholders receive dividends. Choice B is incorrect because capital gains are not usually a factor for bondholders. It is true that if the bond is bought at a discount, a gain may be realized upon redemption, but bonds are also issued at par (face value) or at a premium upon which a capital gain may not be realized. Choice D is incorrect because the expected return on bonds is usually lower than that on the same company's common stock.

10. **The correct answer is C.** When there is net *decrease* in accounts receivable for the period, cash collected from customers is more than *revenues* and would be shown as an increase in cash from operating activities on the cash flow statement. Choice A is incorrect because an increase in accounts receivable would mean that the revenues for the period were more than the cash collected for that period and would be shown as a decrease in cash from operating activities. Choices B and D are incorrect because changes in accounts receivable during a period have nothing to do with expenses.

11. **The correct answer is C.** The insurance costs associated with storing inventory is an example of an inventory carrying cost. Choices A, B, and D are all examples of inventory ordering costs.

12. **The correct answer is C.** The NPV is the net present value of the future cash flows and is found by calculating the present value of the cash flows for year 1 through 4 and subtracting the initial cash outlay ($51,010 – $50,000 = $1,010). If the NPV is positive, the project will be accepted. Therefore, choice C is correct. Choice A is incorrect because $51,010 is not the NPV; rather, it is the present value of the cash flows. Choices B and D are incorrect applications of the tables or the calculations.

13. **The correct answer is B.** The average collection period is calculated by dividing the average balance of accounts receivable by total net credit sales for the period and multiplying the quotient by the number of days in the period (360). It estimates the average number of days it takes a company to collect the cash that it is owed (from its customers) because of credit sales.

14. **The correct answer is C.** Capital budgeting involves using the time value of money principles to discount the future cash flows, including the inflows and outflows as a result of adopting the project. Since options II and III are accrual concepts and may not be representative of cash flows, they are not used in either NPV and IRR analysis where the focus is strictly on relevant cash flows.

15. **The correct answer is B.** The coupon rate is the amount of interest received annually by the bondholder (investor) divided by the face value of the bond ($45 × 2 (semi-annually) = $90 a year; $90 / $1,000 = 9% coupon rate. Choice A is incorrect because 4.5% is based on only one payment per year, whereas this bond pays $45 of interest twice a year. Choice C is incorrect because 10% is based on market value and is the current yield, not the coupon rate. Choice D is incorrect because 10.67% is the approximate yield to maturity.

16. **The correct answer is A.** The comparison of the coefficient of coefficient of variations of these two investments shows that Investment A is less risky than Investment B. When comparing the coefficient of variation of two investments, the larger coefficient means more risk. The coefficient of variation is calculated by dividing the standard deviation by the expected value:

Investment	Expected Value	Standard Deviation	Coefficient of Variation
A	$230,000	$107,700	0.47
B	$250,000	$206,000	0.82

The larger the coefficient of variation, the greater the risk.

17. **The correct answer is A.** The present value of a future amount received in 5 years at an annual interest rate of 10% is $62,090 ($100,000 × 0.6209). When a single amount is discounted into today's dollars, the present value interest factor of a single amount ($1) is used (i.e., the table labeled Present Value of a $1). All other choices are calculated using either the inappropriate table or the wrong number of decimal points.

18. **The correct answer is C.** Since this arrangement is an annuity, the present value of an annuity table must be used. The factor is 3.1699, which is found at the intersection of 4 years and 10%. The present value of a 4-year $20,000 annuity is $63,398 = $20,000 × 3.1699. Choice A is incorrect as it represents $20,000 × 4 (years) = $80,000 of gross or nominal cash flows, but this calculation does not take into account the time value of money (discounting). Choice B is the result of erroneously using the present value factor for a 5-year annuity. Choice D is the result of using the incorrect table (Present Value of $1).

19. **The correct answer is B.** Both options I and II are true. Options III and IV are false statements. The risk of investing in equities is higher than the risk of bonds, and interest rate risk is a concern for bond investors because as interest rates rise, bond values tend to fall, subjecting bondholders to potential capital losses.

20. The correct answer is C. The present value (about $71,000) is found by multiplying the future amount ($100,000) by the appropriate present value interest factor from the table, assuming a 5-year period and an annual interest rate. The unknown amount is the interest rate. By dividing the future value by the present value, you will derive a factor of 0.71. Reading across the 5-year line, you find that the value closest to 0.71 is 0.7130, which is found in the 7% column.

21. The correct answer is D. Revenues, such as sales of products, fees, rent, interest earned and royalties, are reported on the income statement. Choice A is incorrect because accounts receivable, although the result of a revenue event (i.e., sale of a product on credit), are an asset. Choice B is incorrect because not all cash inflows are from the major or central ongoing operations and often, cash inflows are not reported on the income statement. Remember, the income statement only reports cash inflows as revenues if they were the result of a sales, fee, interest earned, etc. Choice C is incorrect because net income is the difference between revenues and expenses.

22. The correct answer is A. Earnings per share is typically reported on the income statement. The balance sheet (choice B), the statement of stockholders' equity (choice C), and the cash flow statement (choice D) are financial statements that do not reveal the earnings per share.

23. The correct answer is B. To discount the $1,000,000 into today's dollars to determine the single deposit into the sinking fund, the present value of a $1 table would be used. You could also the Microsoft Excel PV function or the PV capabilities of a financial calculator to calculate the present value of a future amount. Choice A is incorrect as this is not an annuity. Choice C is incorrect as the future value is already known; the present value must be derived by using the PV of $1 table. Choice D is incorrect because it is not the future value that is unknown, and this is not an annuity arrangement.

24. **The correct answer is C.** The cash cycle is the time period between when a business pays cash to its suppliers for its inventory and when it receives cash collections from customers. Choice A describes only part of the cycle, not the complete cycle in days. Similarly, the inventory period (choice B) is only part of the cash cycle, as is the average collection period (choice D).

25. **The correct answer is A.** To calculate the present value of the bond's future projected cash flows, you must know the amounts of those cash flows (interest and principal/face value), the timing of those cash flows, and the discount rate (the investor's required return). Option II is irrelevant, as the bondholders' other investments and the risks inherent in those investments have no bearing on the value of the bond.

26. **The correct answer is C.** If, after taking into account the beginning cash balance, inflows, outflows, and any minimum cash balance requirements that management has set as a goal, there is a negative number (deficit), then the next section of the budget would show the borrowings needed. Choice A is incorrect because the description given in the question would result in a deficit, not a surplus. If there were a projected surplus, the financing section could show the repayment of any previous borrowings. The concept of net income (choice B) is not based on cash flows. Choice D is incorrect for the same reason as choice B—net loss is an accounting (income statement) concept and is not based on cash flows, but rather revenues and expenses.

27. **The correct answer is A.** Currency risk is risk of loss from fluctuating foreign exchange rates. Inflation risk (choice B) is the risk that rising prices will diminish purchasing power. Interest rate risk (choice C) is the chance that rates of return on investments will be impacted by changes in interest rates. For example, when interest rates rise, bond values fall. Falling bond values impact yields. Liquidity risk (choice D) is the chance that an investment will not be sold quickly and turned into cash without a loss.

28. The correct answer is C. The payback period is the number of years it takes to recover an initial investment in a capital project. When the cash flows are an annuity, the formula for the payback period is initial investment divided by annual cash inflow ($250,000 / $80,000 = 3.125 years).

29. The correct answer is A. The current ratio (current assets / current liabilities) is not used in the DuPont model.

30. The correct answer is C. Hedging is any technique that attempts to mitigate or offset the negative effects of poor investment performance. A leveraging technique (choice A), such as borrowing to invest, is an attempt to boost investment performance but carries additional risk. Speculation (choice B) also carries high risk. Choice D is incorrect because diversification is unrelated to income tax strategies.

31. The correct answer is B. The average tax rate is found by dividing the total income tax owed by the taxable income, while the marginal tax rate is based on the rate of taxes paid on the next dollar of income or the rate of tax savings on the next dollar of deductions. Choice A is incorrect because in this example, the rates are not equal. The only way the rates would be equal is if a person (or a corporation) were subject to a flat tax rate (as the result of tax law). The opposite of choice C is true; Mary's marginal tax rate is 20%, and her average tax rate is 15%. Choice D is incorrect because only the marginal tax rate is 15%.

32. The correct answer is D. The quick ratio is also called the acid test, as it is a more stringent test of short-term liquidity. Quick assets include cash, accounts receivable, and marketable securities and are found by dividing the sum of those assets by current liabilities. Choices A and B are also liquidity ratios but are not referred to as acid tests. Choice C is a solvency ratio.

33. The correct answer is D. The cost of retained earnings is estimated with the same formula as that for common stock. The formula given in choice D represents the dividend constant growth rate formula, one of the possible ways of estimating the cost of common equity. Choice A represents an estimate of the cost of capital for preferred stock that is being issued to raise capital. Choices B and C represent an estimate of the cost of debt.

34. The correct answer is C. The cost of capital is the weighted cost of the components of capital. However, you must adjust the cost of the debt by multiplying the cost percentage by (1 – marginal tax rate) to account for the ability to deduct interest expense from taxable income.

Capital	After Tax Cost	Proportions	Cost of Capital
Debt	7.9%	25%	1.975%
Preferred stock	12.0%	30%	3.600%
Common Stock	15.0%	45%	6.750%
Totals		100%	12.325%

Choice A is incorrect because 7.9% is the after-tax cost of the debt, which is only one component of the capital structure. Choice B is incorrect because 11.63% is the result of a simple average, not a weighted average. Choice D is incorrect because 15% is the cost of the common stock.

35. The correct answer is B. Because this is an annuity, the future value of an annuity factor must be used (14.487 × $10,000 = $144,870). Choice A is incorrect because $166,450 would be the value after the 11th year, and this is a 10-year annuity. Choice C is incorrect as $108,000 is the total of the payments with $8,000 ($100,000 × .08) of interest; however, the interest is earned each year on the balance in the account. Choice D is incorrect because $21,590 is the future value of a single amount ($10,000) as opposed to the future value of an annuity.

36. The correct answer is C. The best estimate of the cost of debt is the after-tax yield to maturity. The coupon rate (choice A) can be quite different from the true cost of a bond, as a bond can be issued at a premium or discount and the real cost of bond must take into account the tax deductibility of interest. A current yield (choice B) is the annual coupon interest divided by the current bond value and does not reflect the amount of funds used by the corporation as a result of the bond issue, nor is the current yield a reflection of the after-tax cost. Yield to maturity (choice C) must be reduced by the tax savings afforded the corporation because of the ability to deduct from taxable income interest expense related to the bond.

37. The correct answer is D. What is described in the question is an ordinary annuity, as the cash flows are assumed to occur at the end of each period ($10,000 × 3.993 = $39,993). Choice A is incorrect because $63,360 is the future value of an annuity due (payments assumed to occur at the beginning of each period). Choice B is incorrect because $58,670 is the future value of an ordinary annuity. Choice C is incorrect because $43,120 is the present value of an annuity due arrangement whereby the payments are assumed to occur at the beginning of each period; the question describes an ordinary annuity with payments occurring at the end of each year.

38. The correct answer is A. Treasury stock is the company's own stock acquired by the company and is reported as negative equity (a reduction in stockholders' equity) on the balance sheet in the equity section. Choice B is incorrect because treasury stock is not an asset of a corporation. Choice C is incorrect as treasury stock transactions do not impact the calculation of net income. Choice D is incorrect as treasury stock is a contra-equity account and is not related to retained earnings or dividends.

39. **The correct answer is B.** Book value per share of common stock is calculated as follows:

(Stockholders' equity – preferred stock) / common shares

($5,000,000 – $500,000) / 100,000 = $45

Choice A is incorrect because $50 is the market value per share ($5,000 / $50), not the book value per share —this is an accounting concept, not a market concept. Choice C is incorrect because $44 is the amount above the par value (an arbitrarily set value) that Jim paid for the stock. Choice D is incorrect because par value is not the same as book value, partly because book value includes additional amounts paid in capital (amounts contributed by stockholders over and above the par value of the stock) and retained earnings.

40. **The correct answer is B.** The expected return of a portfolio is based on the weighted average of the assets in the portfolio. The following is the calculation of the expected return of the portfolio:

Invest-ments	Amount	Expected return of each asset	Propor-tions	Expected return of portfolio
A	$500,000	15%	50%	7.500%
B	$200,000	6%	20%	1.200%
C	$300,000	9%	30%	2.700%
Total	$1,000,000		100%	11.400%

Choice A is incorrect because 10% is the result of a simple average, not the weighted average of the expected returns. Choice C is incorrect as 15% is the return of investment A, but not of the mix of assets in the portfolio, of which investment A is only one of the three components. Choice D is incorrect because 30% is found by summing the expected returns and is not the expected result of the mix of investments.

41. **The correct answer is B.** The balance sheet shows the assets, liabilities, and equities of a business. The question describes an account receivable, a promise from a customer to pay for a sale at some point in the future. The credit terms of 2/10, net 30 mean that the customer can take a discount of 2% if the payment is made within 10 days of the invoice date with the full amount due in 30 days. The statement of cash flows (choice A) summarizes the operating, investing, and financing cash flows in and out of a business during the same time period as the income statement. The account receivable, by its very definition, has not been collected and is not yet a cash flow. The retained earnings statement (choice C) is a summary of the changes in retained earnings during the same period as the income statement, revealing such items as net income (or net loss) and dividends declared. A statement of stockholders' equity (choice D) shows the changes in stockholders' equity during the same period as the income statement, including new issuances of stock, acquisition of treasury stock, and changes in retained earnings.

42. **The correct answer is A.** Slowing down payments without hurting profitability or credit rating is an appropriate working capital management strategy. The strategies presented in the other options will negatively impact the cash conversion cycle. Choice B would result in a quick payment that may not be necessary based on credit terms granted by vendors. Choice C would result in tying up dollars in inventory that may be employed more effectively elsewhere. Choice D assumes that generous credit terms include longer payment periods, which will most likely result in longer collection periods.

43. **The correct answer is C.** This is a lump sum (single amount) and so the Future Value of $1 table must be used ($5,000 × 2.159 = $10,795). Choice A is incorrect because $72,435 would only be the answer if this arrangement were an annuity. Choice B is incorrect as $50,000 is the result of multiplying $5,000 by 10 years; however, the investment is structured with one deposit of $5,000 that will accrue interest at 8% per year. Choice D is incorrect because $5,400 is the future value after one year grown by 8%; however, the question assumes that 10 years of compounding occur at 8% per year.

44. The correct answer is D. The effective annual interest rate is found with this formula:
$$(1 + \text{periodic rate})^{\text{the number of periods in a year}} - 1.$$
The periodic rate on this loan is the quarterly rate of 2.625% (10.5% / 4 = 2.625%). The effective rate is $(1 + 2.625\%)^4 - 1$ = 10.92%. The answer can also be found using the EFFECT function in Microsoft Excel or with a financial calculator. Choice A is the quarterly interest rate (10.5%/4 = 2.625%), but not the annual effective rate. Choice B is the prime rate. This loan's stated interest rate is set based on the prime rate (9% + 1.5% = 10.5%). Choice C is the nominal (stated) rate, not the effective rate.

45. The correct answer is D. Income tax is the last expense listed on the balance sheet, just before the reported net income. Cost of goods sold (choice A) is the first expense on the income statement of a merchandiser or wholesaler. Depreciation (choice B) is deducted before income from operations on the income statement. Interest expense (choice C) is deducted after operating income but before income tax expense on the income statement.

46. The correct answer is B. If you divided the present value of the annuity (PVIFA) by the annuity amount ($42,000 / $10,000), you can derive the present value interest factor for an annuity (4.2). Reading across the 5-year line, you'll find the PVIFA of 4.212 in the 6% column.

47. The correct answer is C. Using the present value tables, the calculation of an IRR is a trial-and-error process. You will find that the NPV of the investment is positive if you try discounting the future cash flows using 10%, 11%, and 12%, which would make choices A and B incorrect, as the IRR is the rate that results in NPV equal to zero. At 13%, the NPV is a negative value (–$209). This means the IRR is between 12% and 13%, which is choice C. The actual IRR (calculated using a financial calculator or Microsoft Excel) is 12.8%.

48. The correct answer is A. If these rates were plotted on a chart with years to maturity on the *x*-axis (horizontal) and the years to maturity on the *y*-axis (vertical), then the line through these data points would be upward sloping, as opposed to flat (choice B), straight across the chart, downward sloping (choice C), or humped (choice D).

49. The correct answer is D. The proportions are as follows:

Component	Amount	Proportions
10% Bonds Payable	$5,000,000	18%
11% Preferred stock	$4,800,000	17%
Common Stock	$12,000,000	43%
Retained Earnings	$6,000,000	22%
Totals	$27,800,000	100%

Equity is the preferred stock, common stock, and retained earnings components (17% + 43% + 22% = 82%). Choice A is incorrect as common stock (43%) is only one component of equity. Choice B is incorrect as 60% only accounts for preferred and common stock, but retained earnings is also part of equity. Choice C is incorrect as 65% is the proportion of common stock and retained earnings to total equity; however, preferred stock is also a form of equity.

50. The correct answer is D. Market prospect ratios, also called market ratios, help investors analyze stock price trends and assist in estimating a stock's current and future market value. The P/E ratio measures the relationship between the current market price of a company's stock and its earnings per share and is also sometimes called the price multiple or the earnings multiple. Times interest earned (choice A) is a solvency ratio. The current ratio (choice B) is a liquidity ratio. Net profit margin (choice C) is a profitability ratio.

51. The correct answer is D. The forward rate is the exchange rate for a future delivery of a currency that you have exchanged, whereas the spot rate is the exchange rate for currency that you are acquiring now. In choice A, the terms are reversed. Choice B is incorrect because spot is the current rate, and bid is the price at which you can currently sell your currency in an exchange. Choice C is incorrect because bid is the price a dealer is willing to pay for currency, while ask is the price at which the dealer is willing to sell.

52. The correct answer is A. The cost of capital for preferred stock that is being issued to raise capital for a firm is found by dividing the expected dividend (for one year) by the net issue proceeds on a per share basis. Choice B is incorrect as preferred stock doesn't pay dividends. Choice C shows the calculation of the cost of a bond, not preferred stock. Choice D shows a way of estimating the cost of common stock.

53. The correct answer is B. The present value of the future stream of cash flows (year 1, $60; year 2, $60; year 3, $1,060) is $923.86 when using the discount rate of 9% (the required rate of return), found this way:

$$(\$1,000 \times 0.772 + \$60 \times 2.531) = \$923.86$$

Choice A is the face value (what the bond will be worth in 3 years), but not its present value. Choice C is only the present value of the maturity value and doesn't include the present value of the interest payments. Choice D is found by dividing the annual coupon payment by 9% (the yield to maturity) and is a rough approximation of the bond value. However, it does not accurately take into account the amount and timing of the bond's cash flows (interest and principal) and is the present value of a perpetuity, which is not this arrangement, as a bond has a definite redemption date.

54. The correct answer is D. The future value of an annuity is found by multiplying the annuity payment by the future value interest factor for an annuity particular time period and interest rate. To find the interest rate when the present value, future value, and years are known, you can divide the future value by the present value to derive the future value interest factor. You can track that factor down in the time value of money table by looking for it on the 10-year line ($724,350 / $50,000 = 14.487). The value of 14.487 can be found in the 8% column.

55. The correct answer is D. The constant growth formula for a valuation of a share of common stock is based on the formula Price $= D_1 /r - g$, where D_1 is the forecasted next dividend, r is the required rate of return, and g is the annual growth rate of the dividend. Therefore:

$$\text{Price} = \$3.00\,(1 + 0.1) / (0.12 - 0.10) = \$3.30 / (0.12 - 0.1) = \$165$$

Choice A is incorrect as $25.00 is based on a zero-growth assumption ($3.00 / 0.12 = $25). Choice B is incorrect because $27.50 is the year 1 dividend divided by the required rate of return; this is the valuation for a preferred stock, not a common stock with a projected dividend growth rate. Choice C is incorrect because $150.00 does not account for the 1-year growth in the dividend.

56. The correct answer is A. The effective rate for this type of arrangement (a discounted loan) is found with this formula:

$$\text{Interest} / (\text{Amount borrowed} - \text{Interest})$$

Therefore:

$$\$9,000 / (\$100,000 - \$9,000) = 9.89\%$$

Choice B is the nominal (or stated) rate, not the rate based on the amount of money the firm could utilize ($100,000 − $9,000 = $91,000). Choice C is the real rate based on the effective rate less inflation (9.89% − 3% = 6.89%). Choice D is the real rate based on the nominal rate less the inflation rate (9% − 3%).

57. The correct answer is B. The break-even point is calculated as follows:

Fixed costs / (selling price – variable cost per unit)

$500,000 / ($60 – $10) = 10,000 units

10,000 units × $60 = $600,000 in total sales

58. The correct answer is D. Corporations conducting business in foreign countries might decide to borrow funds from banks in those foreign counties in the currency of those foreign countries and to finance their operations in those countries. Profits earned in those countries are in the local currency, and the debt is services in that same currency. Paying the debts owed to those foreign banks would be exposed to currency exchange risk if the amounts were paid back in dollars; as is implied with choice A. Choice B is incorrect because the strategy is one to mitigate risk and not to manipulate EPS. Choice C is incorrect because just the opposite is true—the strategy utilizes local currencies (the currencies of the foreign country).

59. The correct answer is C. P/E ratio is Price/Earnings per share; therefore, the price per share is equal to the EPS × P/E ($2.50 × 18 = $45). Choice A is incorrectly calculated as the dividend × P/E. Choice B is incorrectly calculated as the dividend × average P/E ratio of the industry. Choice D is incorrectly calculated as the EPS × industry average P/E, which might be done by an analyst to determine possible upside potential.

60. The correct answer is C. The future value of a single amount (lump sum) is found by multiplying the present value by the future value interest factor for a particular time period and interest rate. To find the interest rate when the present value, future value, and years are known, you can divide the future value by the present value to derive the future value interest factor. Track that factor down in the time value of money table by looking for it on the 5-year line ($28,100 / $20,000 = 1.405). The closet value to 1.405 can be found in the 7% column.

CPSIA information can be obtained
at www.ICGtesting.com
Printed in the USA
JSHW042125200722
28277JS00012B/142